One Does Not Spell Mozart With A "T"

Histerical Dischords in Music

John R. Shannon
FHSA, FAAGO, BS, MA, PhD

Illustrations by
Frank J. Rocca

Hinshaw Music

HMB-141

To My Students

Who, unknowingly wrote the majority of this book.

Library of Congress Catalog Number 83-082777
ISBN 0-937276-05-7

CONTENTS

Chapter I
The Decline of Music in the Ancient World North and South

Egypt and Babblelonia

Our knowledge of music from ancient Egypt is very slight. No doubt we should thank God for small favors. The majority of the evidence for music in these cultures is derived from iconographic[1] sources. The paintings on the walls of the tombs of the ancient pharaohs show many evidences of music. That the dance must have been popular is proven by the many dancing girls in see-through blouses we encounter all over the tombs. By the tenth dynasty the girls are often seen playing harps. No doubt some pharaoh's wife thought that dancing girls with harps were more discreet than dancing girls alone. The harps do not have pedals, and hence do not have to be played in that idiotic key of C-flat major. A trumpet is among the artifacts discovered in the tomb of Tut-tutankamen. The instrument is a straight trumpet without valves, and hence must date from earlier than the 19th century before Christ when Saxankamen was reputed to have invented a chromatic instrument. Without doubt such trumpets were used to blow reveille and taps for the workers on the pyramids. If Egyptian musicians had no more imagination than the architects of those structures, our inadequate knowledge of their music is of little loss.

If we know little of Egyptian music we know less of that of Babblelonia. Recent research with cuneiform tablets has led scholars to believe these ancient people sang in the key of C-major. How this could be, seeing that the Babblelonians had no pianos and hence could hardly have found middle C, had they known what it was, defies explanation. Some scholars will believe anything. There is absolutely no evidence to support the theory that the Babblelonians wrote the melody to the *Star Spangled Banner*. Admittedly it is work of primitive construction, but the official version is in B-flat major,[2] a key we assume had yet to be discovered. In any event, had the Babblelonians written the tune they would have been as incapable of singing it as anyone else.

[1] Iconography is the practice of looking at the pictures and ignoring the text.
[2] Consult the Music Division of the Library of Congress which gets topsy-turvy over all of this.

Music in Ancient Greece

The actual history of western music begins in ancient Greece. No one knows why, but the history of everything begins in ancient Greece, and naturally music must follow suit. Ancient Greek musicians worked very slowly. In over five hundred years of labor they produced only twenty examples of music, and many of these they failed to complete.[3] Originally there was probably more written music, but it was rapidly lost. We know from the descriptions of performances that the choruses in the tragedies of such dramatists as Euripidose were originally sung. Choir members are always losing their music, and this must certainly have been going on in ancient Greece.

Since the composers themselves were so unproductive, the theorists and the philosophers filled in the void. Plato thought music was important, and what Plato thought was important everyone thought was important. Plato believed that the education of the philosopher-rulers should be composed primarily of two disciplines: gymnastics and music. Gymnastics was intended to train the body and music the soul. Just what happened to the mind in all of this foolishness is not clear. The final success of the Romans over the Greeks must partially be explained by the ignorance of the Greeks in matters of armaments, politics, economics, and history. This ignorance we can trace to Plato and his ridiculous theory.

We can also trace to Plato the unfortunate habit of philosophers and rulers of pontificating on just what music the public should be allowed to hear. Plato thought that music in certain modes incited the youth to lurid thoughts. Lurid thoughts are part of growing up, and parents of all generations have had to deal with the problem. Little did Plato dream that music hadn't the least to do with it. From Plato to Hitler someone always tried to suppress perfectly good music which just didn't happen to suit his taste.

Somewhat less dangerous (but only somewhat less) was the work of the Greek theoreticians. One of the most important of them was Pythagorus of right triangle fame. He discovered that the consonant intervals were nothing more than simple numerical ratios. Had he stopped there he would have made an important contribution, but he decided that these ratios were also the key to the universe. Jupiter and Mars were up there humming perfect fifths all the time. Since there was not much music to perform anyway, everyone spent his time trying to hear the music

[3] On an average of every five years, some scholar declares one of the examples to be spurious. In a mere century the fruits of half a millennium will be corrupted. Long live musicology!

Arixtoxenex thinking upside down while a doxtor and nurxe look on.

of the spheres. Concert life in Greece was really dull. Pythagorus did his experiments with hammers of different weights. Imagine how he confused the hardware store owners by coming in, with scale in hand, to weigh all the tools in the Stanley display. Music theorists are weird people.

Arixtoxonex was perhaps the most important of all Greek theorists, and this can be proven by the high level of confusion of his ideas. He shared one particularly absurd viewpoint with other Greek musicians; he simply thought upside down. It was clearly difficult to spend so much time standing on one's head, but since Greek musicians all thought that what was high was low and what was low was high, it was necessary to get into the correct perspective in order even to think. Arixtoxonex invented the tetrachords, and these he got correct. The tone, tone, semi-tome was just as it should be. Unfortunately when he was upside down and connected two tetrachords together, he came down (i.e. up) from E to E and not from C to C. The result contributed, in no small degree, to the woeful lack of tonality in Greek music. Arixtoxonex also described in too great detail the systems of organization of the tones of Greek music: the Greater Perfect System, the Lesser Perfect System, the Greater Imperfect System, and the Lesser Imperfect System. All these systems amounted in the end to the same thing, since they all revolved in circles around the *mesa* A. The lowest (i.e. highest) tone of the Greater Perfect System was added at the last minute and was called the *proslambapotamus.*

From the standpoint of the effect of Greek theory on the history of music, it was its very confusion which really counted. Had the early medievil theorists understood their inheritance (a difficult task indeed in view of the fact its originators didn't understand it either), they might have given up in horror. They then wouldn't have termed the Dorian mode the Dorian, which it isn't; the Phrygian mode the Phrygian, which it isn't; and so on. Theorists love to borrow from the past particularly when they don't understand it in the least.

The favorite instrument of the Greek musicians was the cithara or liar. Legend has it that the first cithara was devised by one of the gods, Apollo or one of those fellows, by stretching strings across a turtle shell. Why gods should go around engaging in such non-productive activity when the universe is in such a hell of a shape is a good question. There was a change in the construction of the cithara when Socrates had the sea turtle placed on the endangered species list.

Music in Ancient Rome

The Romans were always marching off to a war somewhere in their extensive empire. As a

Johannes Phillipus Suetonius, first director of the Roman Army Band.

result, the most important music in Rome was that for military use. The Roman Army Band School was the best in the world. Its director, Johannis Phillipus Suetonius, wrote many marches for the army and moonlighted by directing the circus band in the evenings. An important instrument in the Roman bands was, of course, the tuba which was awkward and heavy to carry. By curving the tubing around the player, the instrument was made more easily portable. The newly formed tuba was called the suetonaphone. Another important instrument developed by the Romans, although it had been discovered in a ruin by the Egyptians, was the hydraulis, or water organ. This was a pipe organ so constructed that it could either make loud music which scared the circus lions into proper behavior or, by forcing water through the pipes, serve as a portable shower for the emporer when he was away from his bath. The hydraulis was very popular well into the Muddled Ages. The eastern emporer sent one to Charlemagne in the eighth century.

Certainly the most famous musician of ancient Rome was the emperor Nero. He took his music seriously, which was only one of his many mistakes. Everyone raved when he sang, just as they did several thousand years later when Margaret Truman sang. If you did not rave, you could expect to be improving the protein consumption of the circus lions. Few critics are honest enough to face that. It is untrue that Nero fiddled while Rome burned. Despite the fact that he certainly attended Suzuki classes, he never mastered the first position.

Chapter II
Music in the Muddled Ages

Medievil[1] music begins with Gregory the Small, pope from A.D. 590 to God knows when. Gregory was a man obsessed, obsessed with doves, whom he allowed to sit on the papal shoulders, and with the notion that everyone, no matter where, should sing just as he did. For many generations the Gauls, the Angles, and those horrid Visagoths had been singing as they damned well pleased, and this His Holiness simply could not accept. At the Abbey of Monte Cassino, south of Rome, the pope founded the FFFFGS.[2] This foundation he staffed with the bureaucrats of his day, men who went around looking severe, wearing long flowing business suits, and who called themselves monks. These monks were charged with three tasks: the first was to determine just how Gregory liked to sing (no easy matter with that omnipresent dove on his shoulders); the second was to write it all down (another difficult task seeing that musical notation had yet to be invented); and finally to disseminate the result throughout the known world (also difficult for nothing annoys people more than to be instructed by others what they should sing and how it should be sung). But Rome being Rome and bureaucrats being bureaucrats they tried, and so we have Gregorian chant.[3]

Because of Gregory's tenacity and also because no one could think of anything else to do with it, his chant became the traditional music of the Medievil Church. Certainly we should thank His Holiness, for if this had not happened, several confusing chapters of Reese's *Music in the Middle Ages* would have been impossible. Those idiotic scribbles we call neumes would have been justly ignored by everyone, and poor counterpoint students would have lacked *cantus infirmi*[4] to serve as the basis for their suffering.

---

[1] Medievil=Latin for in the midst of evil. We must remember these were the dark ages and the sun did not shine for days at a time.

[2] The Foundation for Following Fiercely Gregory's Singing.

[3] Gregory remains the only person in history who lent his name to a significant body of music rather than to the endowment of some library, highway, football stadium, or other monument to utility. But, as we have said, Gregory was obsessed.

[4] Or *canti infirmi,* or *cantus infirmuses,* or *cantuses infirmuses.*

Gregory was so obsessed with the perfection of his own singing that he refused to have any accompaniment. This, no doubt, was a great relief to the Monte Cassino monks who, therefore, did not have to study harmony and counterpoint. They then could spend more time making wine. Women were denied to them; music was their business; and they just had to find some relief somewhere. As a result, Gregorian chant remained monophonic. "Mono-" equals one and "phonos" equals tone. Therefore monophonic equals monotonous. Again we should thank Gregory, because without his chant we would hardly have another example of monophony to burden music appreciation students.

The most important service of the Medievil Church was the mass. The mass received its name from the words used near the end: "Ite missa est." Why it should not have been called the "miss" no one knows. Perhaps the supporters of ERA will take the matter up. Within the mass the most important musical event was the gradual, which received its name because it only gradually came to an end, after which everyone sang "Alleluia." The graduals were very elaborate, too elaborate if you wanted to get home to Sunday dinner and to the Green Bay football game. The singers, but nobody else, enjoyed their performance. Singers always like to show off.

Gregory provided music not only for the mass but for his office. The music for the office was simpler than that for the mass since it had to be done every three hours over the public address system by monks who cared little for singing anyhow. No doubt there were many office petitions to put an end to music for the office. These failed. Gregory was obsessed. As soon as Gregory died, he was buried, but his music lived on to the consternation of practically everybody.

The next figure of consequence was the monk Guido d'Arezzo. Rather than choosing to devote his life to the search for the Holy Grail, Guido decided upon a much more unique quest. He set out to locate among the thousands of Gregorian melodies one which had lines beginning successively on the syllables Do-re-mi-fa-sol-la-ti, which he had learned in grade school. After a decade of conscientious search, he finally located a melody using just five of them. The chant unfortunately began with "ut" and did not use "ti." Imagine Guido's chagrin when he was forced to admit that in no way could "ut" represent a female deer. In any event, this was a peculiar search to say the least, and we must not be too harsh with Guido's partial failure.

From what we can tell, Guido suffered from an unfortunate fetish of the hand. No one could explain why it happened, but everytime the choir sang, Guido was seen up in front pointing with a finger of one hand at the joints of the fingers of his other. No doubt this fetish

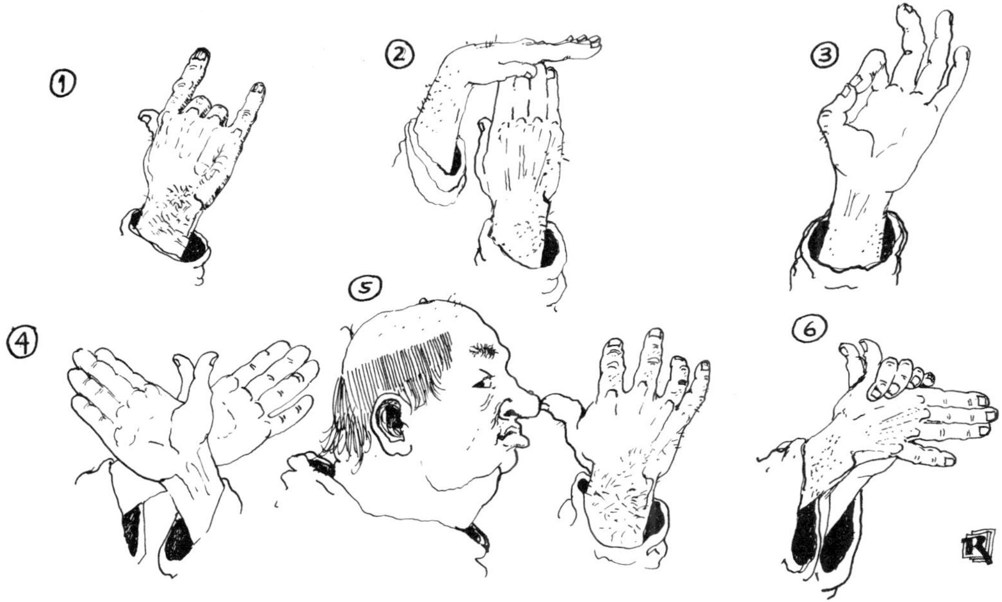

Guidonian hand signs:

1. *"Datta note sounda like-a Hell!"*
2. *"Holda datta note lil' bit-a longera."*
3. *"Atsa sounda pretty okay, datta nota."*
4. *"Pleeza watcha da birdie. He give-a you da right-a note."*
5. *"same-a to you."*
6. *"Looka da cute lil horsey!"*

was the result of his failure in the do-re-mi search, and somehow he felt a sense of relief of his inferiority feelings in his own hand worship.

By far Guido's most important accomplishment was the invention of the musical staff. Only a person with an orderly mind could have done this. We know Guido had an orderly mind because he wrote a music theory text, and only persons with orderly minds do things like that. All those neumes roaming aimlessly about the page were more than Guido could stand, and so he rounded them all up and forced them between parallel lines. How the neumes felt about this we do not know. They had been free for many centuries. The singers hated it because now they had to count their lines and spaces, learn "every good boy does fine", and commit those C-clefs to memory. But even worse was the fact that they now had to sing just what someone else decreed, and singers never like to do that.

By the year A.D. 1000 when the world was supposed to have come to an end but the event was unfortunately postponed, musicians had gotten tired of singing monotonous monophony. Gregory was dead and couldn't defend himself, and thus some bored, young monks invented polyphony.[5] Fortunately, or unfortunately as one might see it, these clever students simply began to sing their chants in parallel fifths. Their theory teachers were aghast, and marked all their papers with endless red feathers. Despite the fact that the students risked failing freshman theory, they persisted. Indeed, they doubled their efforts and thereby added parallel octaves to their already lengthy list of offenses.

Luckily for the history of music, student pranks such as this do not last too long. Soon some contrary student decided to go his own way. The development of contrary motion was an important step in the history of polyphony because now everyone could do his own thing. We all know that is important and democratic. These early examples of polyphony were called *organums* (or *organa* if you like to be precise). No one knows why this term was chosen, but it was necessary to call them something, and that term is as good as any other.

One type of organum practiced by Leonin, a member of the Parisian Ecole des Beaux Arts, was the sustained tone style. The king had a weakminded brother whom he had cast off into the choir of Notre Dame. The king was determined that his brother should have an important part in the musical life of Paris and of the cathedral. Unfortunately the poor man could sing but one tone per hour. For this brother, Leonin devised a style of *organum* in which he could hold his tone

[5] Poly = many and phony = faked. Hence polyphony is music with many faked parts.

The King's weak-minded brother sings the first sustained organum.

until he was blue in the face. Other voices sang quietly above his long tones because the king was determined that his brother should be heard. One notices that the sustained tone *organa* died quickly. The reason for this was that the brother died equally quickly from an unfortunate coronary suffered by holding the same tone for two and one-half hours.

Perhaps the most important contribution which Leonin made was that he invented rhythm. Musicians had been doing well without it all these years, and most of them, no doubt, would have preferred to go along in their stodgy ways. No one has ever liked to practice with a metronome. Leonin organized his rhythm by the modal system which must not be confused in any way with *The Modal System,* which is something altogether different. He used only two note values, long and short, which, unfortunately, he never learned to notate. Instead he connected all his notes together in long ligatures which were too confusing for his singers.[6] It would have been so much simpler if Leonin had understood that a quarter-note is divisible into two eighth-notes. Some learned persons always have trouble with fractions.

Leonin's successor at the Ecole des Beaux Arts was his pupil Perofinn. The king's brother was now dead, and no one else around was interested in sustained tones. Perofinn took it upon himself to write new pieces to substitute for those Leonin had been forced to write for the king's brother. These new pieces, called substitute *clausulae,* were based on an expansion of the *cantus infirmus* technique. This technique is simple: one takes a weak (*infirmus*) melody and adds other stronger melodies above it. Thereby the composer hopes to produce a stronger musical effect than the original melody provided. Out of the *cantus infirmus* technique, as practiced in the substitute *clausulae,* comes the important form of the motet. The term motet is derived from the same stem which give us motley, a word which provides a good description of the form. The strength of the form comes from the fact that everyone who participates sings different words preferably in different languages simultaneously. The cacaphony the motet produces is by far the most characteristic muddling to be found in all of medievil music. We can identify the composers of only a few motets, a fact that is easiest explained by the observation that no one in his right mind would admit the responsibility for such nonsense.

Until the year 1150 most music had been written by churchmen, and, as we have seen, with all too disastrous results. As a result of a decision made by Saint Berhard de nulle Valeur and his

[6] The fact is they are too confusing for everybody except scholars at Yale. Scholars at Yale think they can decipher anything.

A knight, posing as a troubadour, serenades his lady.

consort Helleanor of Aquitaine, the troubadours, trouveres, and minnesingers came into existence. The French couldn't decide what language to speak, and hence they had both troubadours and trouveres. The Germans were satisfied with only German and minnesingers.

The chief subject of the lyrics of these new secular musicians was the court of cultly love. According to the requirements of the court of cultly love, a knight must fall in love with an unattainable lady and stand outside her castle all night in the snow singing lovesongs to her. The popularity of this activity would be hard to explain were it not for the crusades, which were equally as absurd and which occurred at the same time. A knight was given a choice: either he could go to the Holy Land and get a Saracen arrow in his chest or he could go it alone with songs in the snow. Many chose the latter course. Troubadour and trouvere music represented the last great flowering of monophonic music for the simple reason that no professional musician could any longer be induced to participate in such an activity. Only professional musicians could sing polyphony. There is a theory that the court of cultly love existed to control the population explosion within the European nobility. Nothing stems one's sexual ardor more than standing in the snow, playing one's rebec, and indulging in voyeurism by gazing through tower windows.

The minnesingers devised a clever way out of the snow trap. It snows much more in Hamburg than in Avignon anyway, and so they had more of a problem. It would be possible to come inside the cathedrals if the minnesingers directed their lovesongs to the Virgin Mary. No one had thought much about her since Luke completed his gospel, but now she had a purpose. As one lyric of the day put it: "How are you going to keep them out in the snow after they've been warmed in Cologne Cathedral?" As a result, the worship of the Virgin Mary became important at a rather late date. Unfortunately, it was discovered that no Gregorian chants had been written in her honor. The ghost of Saint Gregory was disinterred, and for a while everyone went about writing Marian Antiphons. Soon there were more than enough.

The medievil age was rapidly coming to a close, but unfortunately several more composers were trapped in it. After being a poet and secretary to the king and failing at both occupations, Guillaume Machaut suffered a mid-career crisis and turned to music. His first ambition was to make certain he found a place in the history books. In order to achieve this he undertook the writing of the first polyphonic mass. In this mass he attempted to write for four simultaneous voices when hardly anyone had so far succeeded in controlling a mere three. As a result he wrote many parallel octaves. We should forgive him, however, as he began late in life and never received good theory instruction.[7]

A form in which Machaut did excel was the icyrhythmic motet. An icyrhythm is a starkly cold rhythmic pattern applied throughout a composition to the *cantus infirmus*. By using the same rhythmic pattern over and over the composer was freed from his usual obligation of creativity. He hence could devote more time to devising obscure notations in which to preserve his creations.[8] The icyrhythmic motet preserved the multi-textual and multi-linguistic tendencies of the earlier motets. We might have hoped for improvement, but we must remember we are still in the waning of the muddled ages.

We might also have assumed that the court of cultly love would have died out, but instead of dying it seemed to flourish. Unfortunately the muddled ages had no Kinsey or Masters and Johnson to explain the continuation of the weird sexual aberration. In any event, Machaut provided polyphonic songs in the tradition of cultly love. One of these, *Ma fin est mon commencement* (My End is My Beginning), shows how terribly confused the composer's mind became in his later days. This composition is in canon.[9] A canon was a cryptic rule which provided the solution to obscure notations. Without these canons many pieces of obscure music could not have been transcribed from their obscure notations by obscure scholars writing for obscure periodicals. Now one asks: "would we have been any the worse?" A round is a canon so constructed that the singer gets stuck in a treadmill and can't stop singing. Although we have not mentioned English music before,[10] we must admit that English musicians had constructed a round (the so-called Sumerian Canon) as early as the eighth century before Christ. It is accompanied by a pest in the lowest voices.

We must now travel to Italy. It was a dangerous thing to do this in the fourteenth century because if the black death didn't get you, some family feud would. The first woman composer whom we can identify was Francesca Landini, daughter of the Florentine Duke, Il Grandi Landini. Francesca was an accomplished performer on the portativ organ. Unfortunately some

[7] The result has always been known as the *Mess of Notre Dame*.

[8] Despite the efforts of men like Philippe de Vitry to confuse the matter, a simple and straightforward means of the notation of rhythm had been developed by the year 1325. Composers chose to ignore it. Had they not done so, Willi Apel could not have written more than a quarter of his notation book.

[9] Not to be spelled "cannon."

[10] Much to the relief of the English, no doubt.

members of a rival family made some unseemly comments about her and her organ. *Il papa* screamed: "No bodi-agonna say that my Franny she carry her organo around with her!" He had her critics murdered. Her critics' family had Il Grandi and Franni murdered. As further revenge they covered up the truth about history's first woman composer.

The English composer Dungstable stands astride the gap between the muddled ages and the new period, the Renaissance. We are obliged not to let him fall in, so we will pull him back and treat him in the medievil age. Continental musicians had never relied on their ears. As a result, they relied on university professors who have no ears to tell them about consonance and dissonance.[11] Therefore the French composers had not discovered that thirds and sixths are consonant and that triads and inversions existed. The English had poorer universities but better ears. You can imagine what they found. The beautiful new sounds of English musicians, and particularly those used by Dungstable, impressed their continental counterparts. But they were jealous that they had not given the matter more thought. In a famous poem, *La Déploration à Dungstable,* the writer deplores the use of these new sounds, despite the fact that his colleagues were already using them.

We know little of Dungstable's personal life except that he was interested in roses. In 1432 it is recorded that he won the London rose show with a new hybrid named 'bella'. By now even musicians were tired of being medievil. In literature and the plastic arts the Renaissance had long ago begun, and music was going to be ignored unless it jumped on the bandwagon. The relationship between Dungstable and his younger colleague Dufie was a close one indeed. Dungstable, who realized he had been passed by in the rush out of the muddled ages, advised his friend to: "Go Renaissance, young man, go Renaissance." Dufie took his advice and Renaissance music began.

[11] We must remember that music was treated as a branch of mathematics in the medieval university. At least it was not allied with sociology.

Dungstable composes himself amid his roses.

Chapter III
Music in the Renaissance
or
Who Was in the Delivery Room when Music Was Reborn

By 1450 everyone in Europe had finally agreed that the Renaissance had arrived. There had been a dispute over the matter for well over a century, but now that the Dark Ages were over and the sun was shining regularly even in northern Europe, there could hardly be any doubt left about the matter. Everyone was particularly interested in defining himself in terms of himself, since it was now a firmly held view that the measure of man was man.[1]

Everyone was also interested in getting outdoors and enjoying nature. Nothing is more depressing than being cooped up indoors for a thousand years, and now that nature was greener than ever, it was a pleasant experience. There was a renewed interest in language, particularly in the vernaculars. It was a shock to some to discover that they had been speaking French all those years, and that it might be of some value. As we shall see, an interest in the written and spoken word was an important element in the new musical style.

As we pointed out in the last chapter, the young Dufie was the first composer to sense the new spirit. The iconography of the time shows many examples of out-of-doors music, and Dufie was right out there with everyone else. A peculiar type of music he invented for out-of-doors events was called *fauxbourbon.* These pieces were written especially for the fox hunts of the Duke of Burgundy whom Dufie served. At the conclusion of a hunt everyone would congregate over alcoholic drinks and sing Dufie's latest creations. Dufie observed that persons in states of inebriation do not always sing as high as they imagine. So he cleverly contrived these pieces so that the drunken singers could sing the melody a fourth lower, and everything would work out just fine. The result was a stunning success, and Dufie was allowed to take home any foxes which had been caught. Musicians are always in need of all the economic assistance they can get.

Most of Dufie's important works are masses of a new type. All the movements of such masses are based on the same *cantus infirmus.* Not only was Dufie unable to think of enough melodies for

[1] As usual women were omitted from everything important. No one even suggested the measure of woman was woman.

each movement of his masses, he was often forced to steal from other sources the few he used. One particularly weak song employed by Dufie and other lazy Renaissance composers was the famous tune *L'homme armonique,* a melody which served several centuries later under its English title, *The Harmonious Blacksmith,* as the basis of a series of variations by Handel. Dufie based one of his masses on a chanson he had written, *Se le face y rouge,* a song he wrote after he arrived for vespers two hours late after a particularly riotous fox hunt.

The next composer whom we meet is Johannes Ockeghem, whose name no one, including himself, could spell. Okegham was a composer who kept slipping back into the Muddled Ages despite constant reminders from his friends that he was in the Renaissance. He was most famous for his masses which he often based on unusual compositional techniques. His most famous masses are:

1) The *Missa Caput:* In the *Gloria* the countrapuntal lines became so confused that the composer gave up in distress and shouted: "Das ist Kaput."

2) The *Missa Cuiusvis Toni* (Mass in All the Tones): The composer was unable to decide in which mode to write so he constructed a mass to be sung in all the modes at the same time. The mass anticipates polytonality by five hundred years.

3) The *Missa Prolationem:* A mass so contrived that everyone sings the same melodies at different rates of speed. The singer who finishes first always is awarded a prize.

4) The *Missa Fi-Fi:* A mass based on a *cantus infirmus* derived from the barking of Oceghem's pet dog.

The most important ideal of the Renaissance was balance. The favorite sports of the day were seesawing and working-out on the balance beam. Everything indicates that the universe reached its perfect balance point on January the first of the year 1500.[2] Who should have been alive at this date but the most balanced composer of them all, Joskin de Prey, who in his youth was so balanced that he danced on a cable strung between the two towers of the cathedral at Cambrai. Joskin's method of composition was unique. Since the Age of Science had now arrived, a new type of balance was available which could measure accurately the weight of *brevi, minima,*

[2] The end of the world is obviously set for the year 3000, and, as we have pointed out, not for the year 1000. We have been progressively less balanced since 1500.

and *semi-minima.*[3] When writing a piece, Joskin would carefully weigh the notes of the beginning of a phrase against those in the conclusion of the phrase. The result was perfect balance in his melodic lines.[4]

Joskin's most characteristic works are his motets. Every so often the motet kept popping up when everyone thought he was rid of it. Each time it appeared it was unrecognized because it was never similar to what it had been before. By now the warm sun of the Renaissance had melted its icyrhythms and something had to replace them. Joskin got the idea that if all the voices went around imitating one another no one would miss the icyrhythms, and so the concept of pernicious imitation was born. Joskin also labored diligently to set his texts properly. In one of his motets on the text "I will lift up my eyes unto the hills" he pictured the action in the following manner:

Example W2-1040

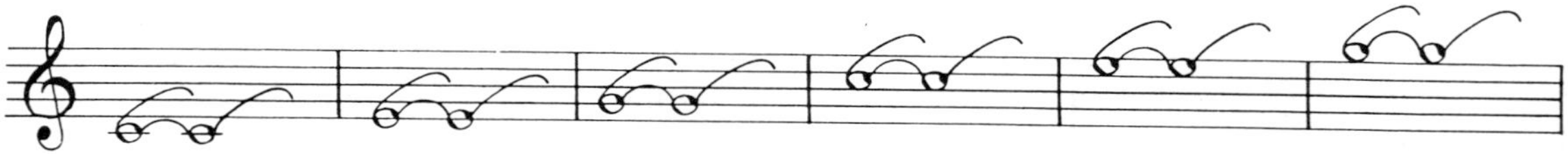

In order to balance this phrase properly he was forced to amend the text by the addition of the words "I will then cast my eyes down into the chasm." Trying to be too balanced can cause trouble.

[3] It was not accurate enough to measure hemi-demi-semi quavers.

[4] It has been said that Joskin solved Ockagham's problem of countrapuntal complexity by his balanced style. Actually he looked the answer up in the back of the book.

Joskin balances on the spires of the Cambrai cathedral.

At just about the time everyone had gotten used to being Renaissance, when everyone was enjoying nature, and when balance was coming along rather well, something had to come along and disturb everything, and that something was the Protestant Reformation. As he tacked those ninety-five theses on the cathedral door, Brother Martin thought to himself, "nothing will ever be the same." And he was right. He had only intended to debate for the rest of his life, but now he was a reformer, and he was obliged to reform. Luther played the lute and thought that everyone else should sing, particularly in church where it would be pious and uplifting. He fancied himself a composer, and he wrote long, slow hymns entirely in whole and half-notes which were called corals. Like everyone else in the age, Luther stole from others. One of his best jokes[5] was fooling people into thinking that barroom tunes sung slowly make pious corals. Luther often had secular tunes modified to suit his purpose. Hence Isaac's infamous melody *Innbruck, ich muss dich lassen* becomes the coral *O Hölle, I muss dich lassen.* All these corals Luther collected and published in the *Witless Gesangbuch* of 1523. Luther also favored polyphonic music and the company of fine composers. He urged Johann Walther to aid him in providing music for the new church. This task must have suited Walther well for he was still active as a composer in the eighteenth century when we know he was a friend of J. S. Bach.

Luther's attitude toward music was positive, i.e. he let musicians largely run their show. It was not so with John Calvin, who as a professional lawyer knew more about religion and music than anyone else alive. Calvin, who couldn't sing, thought that everyone should follow his example. Puritans always make a point of banning only those things which they themselves cannot or do not like to do. Calvin had his congregation singing psalms exactly as the original Jewish congregations had sung them. This was no small accomplishment seeing that no one has ever been able to ascertain just how the psalms were originally sung. But when you are John Calvin, somehow you know. In any event, he instituted monophonic, i.e. monotonous, singing of the psalms, which he now had translated in poetry befitting the monotony of the tunes he provided. Geneva was the perfect environment for musicians of little skill and poets capable of third-rate doggerel. The *Genevan Salter* of 1538 contained only music which was "propre à chanter en l'eglisse." It was not difficult to determine what that was, merely what J. C. said it was. At best the musical style could be termed bourgeois.

[5] Even reformers can have a sense of humor.

In the Anglican reformation, music changed hardly at all. Henry was far too interested in changing wives to bother about changing music. As long as a composer made Henry's current wife happy, there was hardly a musical problem in the realm. Henry's major musical contribution was the making of virginals. Several of them, and a few organs as well, are listed in the royal inventory of 1536.

While northern Europe was getting sidetracked by the Reformation, the Italians had found a new plaything, the madrigal. After a hard day of participating in *vendetti,* the Italian nobles would sit around tables, drink Chianti, and sing polyphonic songs about death, unrequited love, sorrow, and turmoil. It was no wonder that the next day they were ready for some good and honest fighting to relieve their boredom. The madrigal composers were particularly interested in word-painting. Whenever they wrote notes which were blackened, they felt obliged to think of texts that spoke of darkness and of night. Whenever they wrote dissonances which their theory teachers disliked, they justified the dissonance, by words such as *morire.* If they wrote a large number of sixteenth-notes,[6] the verb would be *fugare.* The fact is that madrigal composers always spent much more time fitting the text to music which they had already written than they had spent writing the music in the first place.

The figure whose life best parallels the texts of the Italian madrigals was the professional murderer and amateur musician Prince Carlo Jess Waldo, Duke of Venosa. We are told that the prince loved music above all else, and women he loved not at all. Men like this are better left alone, but a dynastic problem made it mandatory for Carlo to marry one of the loveliest of the Neopolitan countesses. Lady Donna Maria had already put two husbands to shame before she married Carlo, when she was a mere twenty-one years of age. Carlo left her pretty much alone, and that Donna Maria could not stand. Only a few months had gone by before she was in the arms of another and more handsome prince, the Duke of Andria. Carlo was certainly willing to let matters be, had the two lovers not chosen to be indiscreet. One evening when Jess Waldo was having his latest creation performed, they unfortunately laughed aloud at one of his unusual dissonances. Jess Waldo's teachers had tried to restrain him, or at least to prepare him, for the unprepared results of unprepared dissonances. But he wouldn't learn. As a result of the couple's snickering, Jess Waldo became enraged, and that evening he murdered them as they lay abed. For a man to make love to another's wife is one thing; for him to laugh at another's unprepared

[6] Composers always like to write large numbers of sixteenth-notes.

dissonances is just too much. Jess Waldo had the bodies hung outside the castle for all to see what improper resolutions can take place when otherwise consonant persons can take no more dissonance. Thereafter no one, including his theory teachers, dared to laugh at what Prince Carlo wrote. There is some advantage in being a composer who is simultaneously a member of the nobility.[7]

It would be impossible to discuss music in the Renaissance without mentioning the name of Giovanni Pierluigi. His name suggested a member of the Mafia, and, since he worked in the Pope's Sustine Chapel, he chose to use the name of his birthplace instead, Palacetrina. Since Palacetrina worked so closely under the nose of the Pope, it was necessary for him to mind his p's and q's as well as his unprepared dissonances and too striking rhythmic structures.[8] By nature Palacetrina was a timid soul, and it therefore suited his nature to write in a style in which nothing drew undue attention to itself. The Pope could overlook Palacetrina's style for days at a time without even trying.

Foremost in the composer's mind was creating a style which followed so closely the rules of strict counterpoint that when these rules were finally formulated by Jeppesen in 1927, Palacetrina's style followed them immaculately. What a potential disaster for counterpoint students would have occurred had Palacetrina not predicted so accurately what Jeppesen would conclude.

Palacetrina is best known for his masses of masses. One type of mass frequently encountered in Palacetrina's works is the parity mass. In a parity mass, the composer steals an entire movement of another composer and rewrites it in the hope that the new version will be equal in quality (i.e. in parity with) to that which he stole. The result was hardly successful, and the practice made a parody of the art of composition. Even the Pope objected. He pointed out that he was paying for original works, and original works he intended to have. One of Palacetrina's masses, the *Missa Benedetto Marcello,* was reputed to have saved church music. In an effort to answer the musical reforms of John Calvin, the Council of Trent was following him to the letter, and was in the process of banning polyphonic music. Palacetrina wrote this mass for the council, which thought the music so beautiful that it forgot the issue, and church music was saved. We should be relieved

[7] It is not true that the history of opera began in Naples. Thu history of the opera libretto, however, did begin there.

[8] We know that Palacetrina was discharged briefly from papal service. The reason usually given is that he had the audacity to marry. Actually what happened was more audacious. He once tried tc write an unprepared dissonance, and the Swiss Guards caught him in the act.

Palacetrina working under the pope's nose.

that *Roberts Rules of Order* were not in force at the time because someone would have brought the matter up again under the rubric of "old business." Parliamentary order often produces more disorder than we will admit.

Although Palacetrina got all the credit because he followed the rules and behaved himself, Roll and Lasso was certainly the greatest composers of the Renaissance. Palacetrina did not move from Rome. In fact after he got on a tenured track position at the Sustine Chapel, he had little desire to seek a new position. Lasso, on the other hand, was kidnapped three times before he was ten years old, and he kept moving regularly thereafter. He wrote some two thousand compositions dedicated to some two thousand nobles and kings, from whom he was always seeking new employment. He was really caught up in this publish or perish syndrome.

Lasso was a member of a very select fraternity, the Musica Reservata, a society which admitted only the elite of the musical community. Not even Palacetrina was elected. In their secret meetings, they discussed such radical politics as chromaticism, madrigalism, word-painting, and dissonance treatment. In any event, they stayed away from even more radical subjects such as totalitarianism, communism, nationalism, *cantus infirmus* writing, and dominant seventh resolutions. Secret societies should only go so far.

Probably due to his unsettled childhood, Lasso could not determine his country of origin. Therefore he wrote in all the national styles of the day to assure himself that he would hit the proper one. One of Lasso's most important contributions was a set of two-voice motets which have unfortunately provided models of poor writing for every contrapuntal student since the sixteenth century. The least things composers turn out often serve to haunt their memories for centuries. One might feel that Lasso, all in all, had a pretty bad deal, but we must remember he didn't have to put up with the Pope or the Swiss Guards.

Although there certainly was a common musical style in which everyone in the sixteenth century wrote,[9] the composers in Venice had never heard about it. Since Venice is on the wrong side of Italy, it was somewhat isolated from whatever people on the right side of the track were about. The Venetians had to figure things out for themselves, without too much help from anyone including the Pope. Naturally they made mistakes. They got terribly confused about the goals of the Renaissance: being balanced, restrained, pious, and undramatic.

[9] The so-called *prime-evil practtica.*

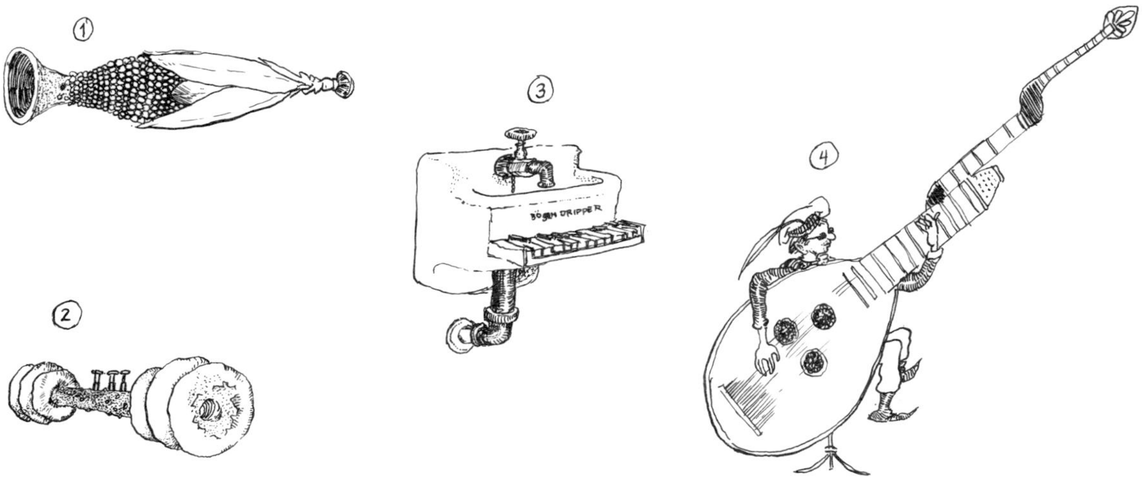

Instruments of the late renaissance.

1. the Cornetto

2. the Bagel horn (not be mixed up with the crumb-horn).

3. the Zink (of which there are two varieties—kütchen and bassruhm).

4. the Theorbabboon or "verye base Lute."

To a large extent the Venetian style hinges on an architectural accident.[10] In the fear that one choir and organ gallery might fall at any time and leave the church without music, the architects of San Marco[11] provided two choir galleries as a kind of musical backup system. The Venetian Musical Union decided it would have twice the political clout if musicians were provided for both galleries. Therefore they had this written into their yearly contract with the Doge.[12] Originally the choirs sang together, but time and again they got out of synchronization. Finally the composers gave up and began writing for them in echo. These separate choruses, the so-called *cori spaghetti,*[13] are the most characteristic feature of the unique Venetian style. It was not long before the idea of two choirs had become a bit dull, and soon a third, fourth, and even a fifth were added. The result was so potentially confusing as to distort the necessary balance of the Renaissance. The practice had become Broque, but no one knew it at the time. We will get to this in the next chapter.

The Venetians were the first to make extensive use of instruments in their music. For years instrument makers had been turning out all manner of wind, string, and keyboard instruments, but nobody had the slightest idea that they could be used to make music. What a delight it must have been when composers found some utility in all those things lying around in the ducal museums. At first, composers simply tried to write motets and madrigals for the newly found instruments, but it was rapidly discovered that instruments couldn't pronounce the words. Hence the forms of *reserchercar* and *canzona* were born. The term *canzona* means song although it was obviously not sung. No one can trust composers to name anything correctly. The Venetian organists, who obviously hadn't been forced to practice Czerny when they were young, now took to doing so in public, and the toccata[14] was born. Another term used for the same form is *fantasia* which certainly points out the fact that these early keyboard players were "out to lunch."

The Venetians could hardly be allowed to get away with all of this without help, so the English jumped in. The English composers began to experiment with their virginals, and it was not long before they were playing variations on them as well. These players were not content

[10] Many architectural accidents are much more unfortunate than this one. No one got killed this time.
[11] That's Saint Marks if you don't want to show off.
[12] The same as duke if you don't want to show off.
[13] Literally "strung-out choirs."
[14] The term derives from the same stem which gave us *tocco* or touched, meaning slightly mad.

with a single virginal but preferred a pair of them, a kind of musical *menage à trois.* Their new style of virginal techniques even intruded into their organ playing in church.

All of this was really getting out of hand. The multiple choruses, the instrumental and virginal playing, as well as the tendencies of the late madrigal were hardly balanced enough to be truly Renaissance. The final blow came, not the Venice, but in Florence. There a group called the *camera obscura* got together to read plays. In a fit of drunken madness they began to sing rather than to read. People had become so unbalanced that the idea stuck, and despite the fact that this new practice was declared a public menace, it was soon taken up by the nobility. Since the nobility itself was already a public menace nothing particular could be done about the matter. All balance had obviously departed; the Renaissance had come to an end; and a new chapter had begun.

Chapter IV
Music in the Broque Era

At the conclusion of the last chapter we pointed out that the balance which was characteristic of the Renaissance was precipitously tottering. Certainly balance is none too common a component of human nature, and for it to have been imposed upon men, to say nothing of women, for over a century and a half was trying at the very least. We showed that in the last years of the sixteenth century forces came into play which threatened the foundations upon which Renaissance music had rested. This was certainly most true in the city of Venice whose foundations were never very secure in the first place. So, then, it was really somewhat of a relief when on January first in the year 1600 the proclamation officially went out: "go for broque."

Everyone had been restraining his emotions all these years in order to obtain balance. Now that hope for balance had vanished, passions came to the fore. The new aesthetic goal was emphasis on emotions. Everyone went around acting as emotional and passionate as possible. The number of duels shot up alarmingly as did the birth rate. Since everyone went around in tears most of the time,[1] the manufacturers of handkerchiefs showed a handsome profit. In the visual arts, it made little difference if a painting or statue showed any competence of craftsmanship. All that was necessary for a work to get an "A" was that it show intense and personal emotion.[2]

The Papacy, which was absorbed with the Romantic side of this new movement,[3] turned the control of the church over to the Jesuits, who got their kicks by lopping off the heads of every non-Christian they could find. They had a particular predilection for Jews and Indians, both of whom just didn't seem to fall properly in line. Since either Jews or Indians could be found almost anywhere, the Jesuits had adequate sources for passionate expression. When these sources dried up, the Jesuits founded colleges which taught complicated theology, which the Jesuits themselves didn't believe, and had excellent football teams which prayed before every game.[4]

---

[1] Laughter and happiness were never regarded as true Broque emotions. This in itself shows much about the nature of the period.

[2] This idea is accepted by undergraduates to this day.

[3] After all these years the Pope finally discovered girls.

[4] Some good comes out of nearly everything.

The Germans, who are always prone to carry excess to excess excessively, started warring amongst themselves in 1618, and they managed to keep passions heated for thirty years.[5] The Germans certainly got the prize for the longest passion in history. They were so taken with themselves that they kept the Broque Era going for a half century longer than anyone else. In fact, they managed to boil the whole thing down to a set of rules, the so-called *Affektenlehre*, the law of the affected. In no other musical area did this law apply so thoroughly as in the field of opera, to which we now turn.

Opera

Certainly the most characteristic medium in which Broque composers expressed their new found love of passion was in opera. As we pointed out in the last chapter, opera had sprung from the madness of the Florentine *camera obsura*. Failure of the civil authorities to quell this disturbance led inevitably to its being accepted as a civil adornment, and from that time to the present it has remained out of control. The term "opera" simply means "work" and is derived from the fact that it demands the greatest work from everyone involved: composers, singers, designers of stagecraft, dramatists, and, most of all, the audience. In fact the medium is better understood by using the term employed in the early seventeenth century *trauma per musica*.

As the Broque progressed, opera split into two types, *opera seria* and *opera buffa*.[6] Unfortunately there was no way to tell the difference between the two since *opera seria* is certainly the Western world's greatest comedy, and *opera buffa* apes *opera seria* as closely as it can.[7] The best clue one can get is to read one's program as you enter the hall.

Broque opera is carefully divided into scenes, each made up of a recitative followed by an aria. In a recitative the singers sing just exactly as they talk in real life. If that is how they talk in real life, perhaps all of them should be institutionalized. During the recitatives the keyboard player sounds occasional chords to keep the singers on pitch and to keep himself awake. Finally the continuo player plays an authentic cadence to indicate to the singer he should move on to the aria. The authentic cadence is the only authentic part of a recitative. Since the type of recitative

[5] As you might imagine the Thirty Years War ended in 1648 with all the participants agreeing to the state of affairs as they had been in 1618.

[6] Simply serious and comic opera if you don't want to sound learned.

[7] Mozart, the greatest opera composer of all, finally gave up trying to make the distinction. If he couldn't figure the matter out, no one could.

we have just described leaves all its participants and the audience in desperate need of a drink, it is called *secco* or dry recitative.[8] The purpose of the recitative is to advance the plot, but since most Broque operas hardly have any plot, recitatives could fairly be eliminated. In any event all recitatives sound alike unless one understands Italian. Perhaps even if one understands Italian, they all sound alike.

It was in the arias that the singers had their most important days in court, and considering the manner of singing, the jury should have found them all guilty. In the first place there was little relationship between the notes which composers wrote in their arias and the notes the singers sang. In fact an authentic case exists in which the orchestra played one aria, the singer sang another, and no one, least of all the composer, knew the difference. All this improvisation merely revealed one thing, singers never can read music. In the second place most Broque arias were accompanied by obbligato instruments. An obbligato instrument is one whose player cannot take a coffee break until the aria is over. There was supposed to be a connection between the music played by the obbligato and that sung by the singer. Just what that connection was was rarely defined.

The most advanced Broque arias are of the *da capitated/ ritornello* type. A *da capitated* aria is one which the composer cannot complete so he merely jumps back to the beginning and goes over the same material again. In a *ritornello* the music merely dances some more around the mulberry tree. During the aria, the action of the plot comes to a complete standstill. But, as we observed, the plots were none too thrilling anyway. In one opera, the heroine is being strangled to death by her jealous husband. Jealous husbands are present in all Broque operas. At this point the singer sings an aria about how painful it is to be strangled. Just exactly how she was to supposed to have gained wind to express this lofty sentiment is unclear, but remember this is opera and an aria.

Another aria form used frequently by Broque composers is the groundout bass type. Here the composer thinks up a short bass line which he repeats *ad nauseum* until the aria is over. This form is unmatched in its ability to depict the effect of sheer and complete boredom. Nonetheless some of the most beautiful moments in all opera are built over groundout bases. Good composers seem to be able to transcend almost anything. One type of groundout bass line used to

[8] There is also another kind of recitative called accompanied recitative, but since *secco* recitative is also accompanied, just exactly what the difference between the two might be is not clear.

An opera heroine being strangled while singing her aria . . . or is it an opera heroine singing her aria while being strangled. Oh Hell! The results were the same.

express grief employs descending, chromatic motion. The most famous example of this lamentable bass occurs near the end of Purcell's opera *Dido and Aeneus.* Dido sings her famous aria as Carthage burns in the background. As the heat rises, the waxen wings of her courtiers melt, and the opera ends with the famous setting of "With Drooping Wings." Another name for the groundout bass is the *basso astinato.*

Now that we have explored the nature of aria and recitative, we must now explore the nature of the singers, a matter of no little delicacy. In Broque operas the women were straight, or at least straight enough not to endanger the biological future of the human species. The heroes, however, were something else. All of them had been "taken to the vet" early in their pubescences and, as a result, they screeched alarmingly from then on. Who wouldn't! Nonetheless, a world which would give credence to opera in the first place would have had little trouble in accepting heroes who sang soprano. It was the heroes themselves who had trouble accepting the practice and you can see why. Many of the *castrati* were favourites of the countesses of the day. It says a bit about the ignobleness of the nobility of the day. Despite their early Industrial Revolution, the English did not produce *castrati.* Instead they imported them along with entire operas and composers. The French, of whom *bon gout* was required, would have nothing to do with *castrati.* Instead they invented ballet.

There were, of course, a few members of the nobility who had discretion, good taste, and plain common sense sufficient to allow them to avoid opera altogether. For these courts composers created opera which was not opera and called it chamber cantatata. Chamber cantatatas use the same forms as operas but have the advantages of being shorter, far less excrutiating, and certainly less expensive. The church, which from time to time looked aghast at the stage, nonetheless had to have its own opera which appeared under the alias of oratorio. Texts for oratorios were stolen from the Old and New Testaments, less frequently from the Apocrypha, and never from the Koran. Although oratorio used the same recitatives and arias as did opera, there was a narrator which told you what was going on, if you wanted to know. Oratorios were almost never staged since all the technical skill available to the church was being used by the Jesuits to devise more exquisite tortures by which the gospel of Christ could be promulgated. The Jesuits never caught on that in oratorio and its parent form, opera, they had available a torture sufficient to make the most impious heretic cry "Lord have mercy" by the end of the first act.

Finally we should say a word about the instrumental music in opera. The overtures were musically the best parts, since they had not the slightest thing to do with the operas to which they were attached. The fact is that many members of the audience listened attentively to the overture and spent the remainder of the evening drinking wine and eating spaghetti right in the middle of the opera house. Some persons are intent on preserving their sanity no matter how strong peer pressure may be to do otherwise.

Instrumental Music

Meanwhile composers working in the field of instrumental music had not been lazy. The technical developments in instrument building in the Broque were impressive. The vile viols of the Renaissance had given way to the violin family which in turn gave way to the Stradivari family. The crummy crummhorns of the Renaissance had now been replaced with oboes that no one could play in tune. The easy-to-play recorders were given up in favor of impossible-to-play traverse flutes. The virginal virginals were given up in favor of two manual Flemish harpsichords in which the same keys of the two manuals didn't play the same pitch. Numerous arguments about how to tune these instruments took place. The old evil-tone temperament of the Renaissance was given up in favor of a host of new temperaments, all more or less out of tune but each claiming to be more in tune than all the others. The goal was to be able to play equally well in all keys, although most musicians got hopelessly lost when key signatures exceeded two sharps or two flats.

The most important form of Italian instrumental music was the gross concerto which was composed most often for stringed instruments and continuo. Before we get to the description of the concerto itself, the continuo, which plays such an important place in Broque music, must be explained. The unfortunate continuo player was a keyboardist who had been provided with a score which the composer had not, or perhaps could not, finish. The player was forced to make up his accompaniment based on a series of numbers provided for him. If he had failed first grade arithmetic, the player was just lost, but then the string players were probably lost anyway so it didn't make too much difference. The continuo player was always doubled by a cellist or a bassoonist under the assumption that if one got lost the other could get him back on the track. Although the author of his definitive biography does not mention the fact, one of P.D.Q. Bach's most important works, *Das schlecht Art das Continuo zu Spielen,* deals with the art of improvising from figured bass.

Now to return to the grossness of the concerto. The concept of the form is simple: a large group of players, the *tutti frutti,* declare war on a smaller, more vulnerable group, the *concertina.* The odds are always one sided as everyone understands. The point is, however, to see how long the small group can last before giving up and finally going along with the crowd. The rules are even more one sided, since the *tutti frutti* get to play the same old thing everytime they get the ball while the *concertina* must think of something original. Brownie points, however, could be scored by the *concertina* if it were able to play more than six straight pages of sixteenth notes without stopping. The frenzy had to be experienced to be believed. The game was divided into two halves separated by an aria, although to the relief of everyone, it was not sung.

The Italian composer Vivaldi got in a rut writing these pieces, and before he knew it he had turned out over five hundred. J. S. Bach, was, however, more discreet. He settled for a set of six dedicated to the Margrave of Brandingiron who neglected to have them played. Bach, then, never knew how they sounded. One modern performance used a soprano saxophone in lieu of the required trumpet. Bach did know he didn't want that.

Bach's other contribution to the gross concerto was his dismissal of the *concertina* players and his replacing of them by the solo harpsichord. You can guess who was playing the harpsichord. No one paid much attention so Bach tried two harpsichords with Wilhelm Friedemann helping out. Still nothing happened. He called K.P.E. and tried three instruments. Still no results. Finally Johann Christian was summoned, and four harpsichords sounded forth. With this the performers caught the Archduke's attention because there is is no way four harpsichords can be made to play in tune. It was fortunate the matter ended here because Bach had run out of musical sons.[9]

In Germany during the Broque, most keyboard players played the organ at least on Sunday to pay for Saturday night's beer. Lutheran services regularly lasted for five hours, and few pastors could preach that long, although some tried. The time that was left over was devoted largely to music. German organists took themselves very seriously and were very important particularly if their surname was Bach. The census of 1680 revealed that seventy-three per cent of all German organists were named Bach and that constituted a large number of important persons. Those unfortunate persons named something else had to settle for being pre-Bach composers. Of these Boxtahund and Packabell were the most famous.

The organs played by these musicians were the most splendid instruments ever built. The

[9] No mention is made by Forkel, when he related these events, of the presence or absence of P.D.Q. The fact is, Forkel, who had too much sense, never mentioned P.D.Q. Biographers should leave some skeletons in the closet.

Boxtahund playing on the pedals.

Grossorgel was always surmounted by an *Oberorgel,* which was surmounted by a *Hochoberorgel,* which was surmounted by a *Hochestoberorgel,* which was surmounted by a cymbelstern. The cymbalstern was made of little bells which the organist could sound when five hours was finally up and his union allowed him to leave his organ bench. Behind the organist stood another small organ, the *Rucksackorgel* which had a sound similar to that of the peasant bagpipes. To play all these divisions at one time was a feat requiring hands and feet of no small ability. Boxtahund, who invented the long pedal solos characteristic of Broque toccatas, was the first to use the expression: "look, Ma, no hands!" It is reported that one Hamburg organist, while playing one of these solos, slipped and fell into the pedal board. The resulting din rendered him permanently deaf.

The organists needed something to use as the basis for their music so they turned to the corals, which everyone else had been trying to forget since the days of Luther. Organists are by nature conservative, and they keep digging up music everyone else had hoped would be permanently buried. The Lutheran organists invented a form known as the coral prelude. The goal of this form is to use the notes of the coral in such an arcane way that they are completely obscure and could not possibly be recognized. To avoid boredom and the embarrassing in-church nap, many Lutheran congregations engaged in contests every Sunday morning. Parishioners were encouraged to guess which tune the organist had used in his coral prelude. Although there were rarely winners, the prize was desirable. If a person won, he was relieved of his obligation of attending the next Sunday's service. Boxtahund was a master at obscuring the coral. He forgot to write the title on the manuscripts of three of his pieces, and musicologists still argue about which corals were used in them.

Another form of insanity in which the Lutheran organists engaged was the fugue, a word which is derived from the Latin word for flight. It would have been all right had all fugues been flighty, but unfortunately they were all too serious. It was their hearers who took to flight, if at all possible. In a fugue a single subject is played by each of the voices at different times, and just to keep the thing together is no easy task. To understand all that is going on requires a knowledge of musicological pathology beyond the ken of most music lovers. Sometimes some voices play the subject twice as fast as it should go and others twice as slow. Such demented and augmented performances add further complexity to the already complicated structure. At other times one of the voices, generally the bass, just tires of everything and holds a single note until he can relax. At other times all the voices climb one over another in a fashion that is called *stretto.* Narrow is the way and strait is the path that leads to the understanding of the fugue. Broque composers often introduced their fugues with preludes. The idea was apparently that their audiences should be prepared for something. Just what was not made clear.

One would have thought that the poor German burgers would have been reduced to ground meat by this conspiracy between the organists and the clergy. But no! The sado-mechanistic strain of the German mentality won out, and yet another musical trauma was added to the Lutheran service, the cantatata. The church had quite rightly preached vehemently against the abomination of opera. We could have taken the clerics seriously had they not then appropriated everything that was opera into the cantatata. A cantatata is nothing more than a short, i.e. less than five hours, opera on a sacred, but not too sacred, text. In order to make these affairs sound a bit more churchlike, the choir sang long choruses based on corals. These things keep popping up everywhere they don't belong.[10]

In order that our reader can understand just where all this could lead, we must recount here an incident which took place in Leipzig during the first performance of Bach's Cantatata Number 140. During the second duet the bass and the boy soprano began to take the text "O, I am Thine and Thou art Mine" too seriously. The duet came to a pianissimo end as its two participants sneaked quietly behind the *Grossorgel* case and continued behind the *Hintersatz.* Hastily Bach launched into the coral "Sleeper's Wake" so that all who were napping would not miss the fun. After Bach's death, cantatatas were banned at Saint Tommy's church. The Leipzig burgers had had too much spice in their mustard.

In the area of secular keyboard music, things had been moving rapidly. As soon as the harpsichord players had solved their temperature problems and found out how to tune two manuals of their harpsichords to the same pitch, a feat accomplished by the year 1700, composers began to write French sweets by the pound. It may be that the incongruities of French sweets may turn the reader a bit sour, but nonetheless they must be explained. In the first place, French sweets are made of dances which are not intended to be danced to. In the second place, they were often written by such German composers as Bach, who were too Lutheran to dance. And finally, although they were French in style and written by Germans, they were often called English. Perhaps this is what the famous music historian Bukofzer meant by the confusion of national

[10] The choirs of Bach's day did not use church sopranos, but something even more horrible: incorrigible brats who sang soprano. The life of a church musician has never been an easy one.

styles. Many of these sweets opened with overtures similar to the overtures to operas. What a relief it must have been to the audience when the second movement was a dance instead of a recitative. The first dance in a French sweet was usually an Allemande, which meant German. Then came the courante, which was Italian; then the sarabande, which was Spanish; the minuet, which seemed to belong to everybody; and finally the sweet ended with a jig, danced by British seamen. Not a real French thing in it, but then again the French are always claiming something they don't own, like Indo-China. As long as anything was flavored with *bon gout,* a spice which cannot really be appreciated unless you were born in Paris, it could be claimed truly French.

Broque Harmony

Until the Broque, composers hadn't paid too much attention to harmony. They had allowed harmony to take place more or less accidentally, and, as anyone who has common sense can see, that method is likely to produce little harmony and many accidents.[11] Broque composers, however, discovered that chords made sounds, an observation that seems to have escaped composers in the past. It is true that Renaissance composers had introduced dissonances into their works as gourmet cooks introduce spices into their cooking. You know they are there, but no undue attention is called to them. Broque composers, however, discovered that dissonances could sound annoying in and of themselves, and, if used in combinations of one another, could produce some fairly excruciating moments, moments appropriate to such passions as death, unrequited love, and Jesuit theology. Monteverdi risked being called before the Inquisition for using a dominant seventh chord without preparation. He defended himself by claiming he hadn't realized it was a dominant seventh, since nobody was yet teaching a freshman harmony course, and besides, he said, he resolved it properly. Other composers invented the diminished seventh chord, which is made up of the drunken combination of two diminished fifths. Another chord used very often by opera composers was the Napoleonic sixth chord. The Emperor was charmed a century later when he discovered that the Italians, whom he had just conquered, had had the foresight to name a chord in his honor.

Some Important Broque Composers

Monteverdi

Claude Monteverdi, or Greenberg if you wish, was the most important composer of the early

[11] This attitude toward harmony is still characteristic of first year theory students.

Broque. The Broque conveniently divides itself into early, middle, and late, and if you were unlucky enough to be born before 1620 you had to be early. What Monteverdi thought about this we don't know. It has been said that if a genius such as Monteverdi had not come along when he did, opera would have died a just death. In view of his beautiful music, we must forgive the composer this one sin, even if its implications were staggering for the subsequent history of music. Monteverdi kept losing his scores, or using them to set fires or to stuff around the contents of packages he was sending. As a result we have only three of his operas today. One of these, *The Coronation of Poppea,* is about the Roman emperor Nero who doesn't get a chance to fiddle, on the fiddle that is, in over a hundred pages of music. Perhaps Monteverdi knew how poorly the emperor really played. It is a relief that the Moral Majority has not yet discovered this libretto. Nothing in Penthouse magazine is that pornographic. The final duet of the opera is its most famous piece. Unfortunately one cannot tell which singer is Nero and which is Poppea, his mistress. They are both sopranos. Monteverdi seems to have had the last word about both Nero's musicianship and his masculinity.

One famous event in Monteverdi's life concerns his argument with the famous music theoretician, Obtusi, whose famous volume, *The Impoerfections of Modern Music* (1600), attacked the composer scurrilously for his unprepared dissonances. These dissonances, said Obtusi, were so harsh the ear was offended rather than delighted. Further, he said Monteverdi ignored the rules of the composers of old, and the result was only confusion and imperfection. Obtusi's observations were precisely correct, only ill-timed. He suffered from being three hundred and fifty years too early. Prophets are never appreciated in their own time.

Purcell

The life of the English composer, Henry Purcell, was one misfortune after another. In the first place, half his acquaintances pronounced his name one way and half another. Perhaps Purcell didn't care, but it may have caused him an identity crisis. In the second place, the English didn't like music written by Englishmen. It simply didn't sound foreign enough. The composer was forced to copy from both the French and the Italians to have any chance at all. His critics said his sweets were not sweet enough and his fantasys were not fantastic enough. The English have always been hard to please. Purcell's final tragedy was that he earnestly wanted to write operas, and the English would allow him only to write incidental music to one incident after another in such children's plays as *King Arthur* and *The Fairy Queen.* Finally Purcell found a girl's school which was willing to risk an opera. Girl's schools will risk anything to get in the news. As a result, we have *Dido and Aeneas,* which we have already mentioned. The opera was doomed from the beginning. In the first place, it only lasted for one hour, and, as anyone knows, no opera can be deemed a success if it lasts less than five hours. In the second place, Purcell, who knew no Italian, insisted on writing in English. He had simply not discovered the fact that opera composition never requires knowledge of the language you are setting. In any case, any opera which the audience could understand was further doomed. Purcell, who was once quoted as saying that it required no particular genius to write in ground-out bass forms, uses them in well over half the numbers of this opera.

Perhaps Purcell suffered from an inferiority complex, one no doubt justified by the treatment he suffered at the hands of his native countrymen. In any event, he died young, and his death set the stage for the importation of Italian opera into London. What the English can't manufacture, they import. Italian opera just didn't lend itself to the factory methods of the Industrial Revolution. Actually it didn't lend itself to much else either.

Johann Sebastian Bach

Some confused student once wrote of the life of Johann Sebastian Bach: "Bach was born in 1685 and died in 1750. He had twenty-three children and kept an old spinster in the attic on which he practiced." The statement is grossly inaccurate. He kept no spinster, only a virginal, in the attic. The young Bach was certainly musically precocious. He may have been sexually precocious as well. Spitta relates the story that Bach's older brother, who was then the young composer's guardian, kept a volume of the works of Packabell carefully locked in a cupboard downstairs. The young boy would sneak down from his famous attic, pick the lock of the cupboard, and copy the contents of this sacred volume for himself. How do we know that his older brother did not keep an entire file of *Spieljunge* also locked up in this cupboard?

The family of the young Bach was simply filled with musicians and with Johanns. Everyone was named Johann: Johann Christoph, Johann Michael, Johann Ambrosius, Johann Bernhard, Johann Nickolaus, Johann Jakob, Johann Ernst, and so forth. What a fate for a young lad: to be a musician and to be called by one's middle name. After a student apprenticeship as a choir boy in the city of Lueneberg, where young Sebastian did as much mischief as his classmates but got paid more for doing it, he became organist in the town of Arnstadt. He soon lost his job there because his corals confused the congregation; when he had neither tenure nor the protection of a first class union, he took an extended vacation to visit Boxtahund; and because he brought his kissing cousin, Maria Barbara, into the church at night for some organ practice. He soon had another job at a place called Mulehousen, but he didn't keep that too long either.

After these two fiascos, Bach settled down at Weimar to hold a job. The three positions he held during the remainder of his life correspond to the three creative periods in his composition. All composers should have three creative periods, never more and rarely less. At Weimar he served the Duke Wilhelm Ernst as earnestly as possible. Here Bach made a reputation for himself as an organ virtuoso. When asked about his skill, he made light of it. "All one must do is to play the right notes at the right time and the instrument does the rest," Bach said. Most organists have been trying to do that unsuccessfully ever since.

The Duke liked Italian gross concerti, and Bach took to liking them very fast. Since he couldn't think of any of his own, he transcribed examples from other composers. One of these composers, Johann Ernst, was the nephew of the Duke. Why do you suppose Bach chose him? In any event it didn't profit Bach much. Johann Ernst was from the side of the family that no one mentioned, and Bach discovered this fact too late.

It was during his Weimar period that Bach journeyed around the country playing all the new organs he could find. On one of these trips it was arranged that he should engage in an organ playing contest with the French composer and organist, Louis Marchand. Unfortunately when the time came, the Frenchman was nowhere to be found. Marchand knew when to march on when the marching was good.

After four years at Weimar, Bach became itchy to leave, particularly after he was offered a job at four times the pay. Duke Ernst said Bach couldn't leave; Bach said he was going to. The Duke had Bach arrested and put in a cell with a single volume of music paper. Since he hadn't written any corals lately, Bach decided to write two-hundred and fifty of them. Had Bach finished this work it would have been entitled the *Grossorgelbuch.* Ernst, however, relented when Bach had finished only forty-three corals. As a result, the work has been known ever since as the *Orgelbuechlein* (The Organ Pamphlet).

Bach's next position was as chambermusician to Prince Leopold of the Duchy of Coethen. The court of Leopold was Calvinist in faith and hence the church had no use for music. Bach was relieved. Now he could write sweets, sonatas, and harpsichord music to his heart's content without ever thinking about corals or cantatatas. Not only did he get paid well for doing what he liked, but his patron was a good musician and played the vile viol less than vilely. All was a veritable bed of roses. His older sons were showing immense musical promise, and P.D.Q. hadn't been born yet, a certain relief to the elder Bach. The composer's only sadness was the death of his first wife, but after mourning her for six months he married a good looking and much younger opera singer with an excellent part-time job. Anna Magdelena bore him thirteen children or thirteen and a half if you count P.D.Q. Bach wrote a musical notebook for his new wife into which he twice copied Gerhardt's famous hymn, *Gib dich zufrieden und sei stille* (Just be Satisfied and Sit Still). Bach had an unreasonable attitude toward a mother of from thirteen to thirteen and a half kids. All would have turned out well for Bach had he not decided to give up a perfectly fine job for a positively lousy one. Not writing corals seemed to have bothered Bach's Lutheran conscience, and so he returned to the field of church music with all the problems that brought.

The final position Bach held was as *Kapellmeister* at the Church of Saint Tommy's in Leipzig. If you are a church musician, everyone thinks he is your boss. The situation at Leipzig was different. There everyone *was* Bach's boss. Everything turned wrong. Bach had slid six rungs down the social ladder; his salary was one-quarter what he was used to;[12] his wife couldn't work since women could not sing in church; and finally, he knew the church didn't really want him but wanted instead the two incompetents who had had sense enough to turn down the job before he arrived. On top of all of this, Bach was required to teach Latin, a task which is difficult enough at best and practically impossible if you don't know anything but *quid pro quo*. But anyway, Bach had managed to escape Coethen, where he had been happy.

The majority of Bach's time at Leipzig was spent in writing cantatatas (over three hundred) and letters (over five hundred) to the town council, to the church consistory, to the Elector, and to anyone else who would listen to his woes. It seemed that every time Bach complained about his salary, which was every month, his salary was cut. P.D.Q. arrived on the scene and money had to be spent for psychiatric counseling (for the elder Bach, that is). The choir boys were always carving graffiti on the choir stalls. Some of this suggested that Leipzig would be better off with another musician, a fact that had not escaped many of the elders. The organs in the two churches he served weren't even in the same key. And besides, the university where he served part-time didn't allow him tenure because he didn't have a doctorate. The university preferred a musician named Goerner, who, Bach said, should have been a cobbler. This poor fellow had a justly

[12] Bach kept praying that parishioners would die so that he could play for their funerals for his fee. He may have prayed that others would die for even more earthly reasons.

deserved inferiority complex. He was inferior. He had to play the organ while Bach conducted, and Bach said of him, with justice, "he never plays any of the notes at the right time."

In the last ten years of his life Bach drew further and further away from active musical life, and the Leipzig burgers drew further and further away from him. Bach set about writing huge collections of music which only he understood and which only he could play. At the time of his death, he was at work on one of these, *The Art of Fugue*. In this work a single subject serves as the theme for innumerable fugues. Even Bach could survive only nineteen of them before terminal illness ensued. At his death there were few mourners. The town council was happy it no longer had to read all those letters, and the choir boys were happy they didn't have to master all those complicated soprano parts. Poor Barbara didn't even get the master's complete annuity, but she did retain custody of P.D.Q. Bach's life at Leipzig was summed up by one town official: "I suppose he was a good composer. But he was a lousy schoolteacher." People want musicians to be everything to everybody.

Handel

Georg Frederick Handel (you can spell each of these names in at least two ways) was born of strong Germanic stock (i.e. his father was a barber/surgeon with a strong stomach) in the city of Halle. Although Handel was born in the same year as Bach not far from that master's birthplace, the parents of the two young geniuses had sense enough to keep them apart. Handel's father wanted his son to be a lawyer anyway, but the Duke intervened as dukes are wont to do. It was too bad parental advice was not followed because Georg Frederick would have been rich much sooner, and he would not have had to throw opera singers out of second floor windows. The Duke's advice won out as duke's advice is wont to do, and the young Handel was sent to study music with the famous musician Zachacow, famous that is if you lived within five miles of Halle. From his teacher Handel received a thorough training in organ playing, Germanic counterpoint, and fugue. Notwithstanding these liabilities, Handel was still able to become a good composer.

In 1703 the young Handel began his creative career in the Venice of the north, Hamburg. The city had all the advantages of its southern model and one didn't have to keep falling into those damn canals. The wise Hamburgers had established their opera house in the Goose Market,[13] where it rightfully belonged, and one egg after another had been laid there until

[13] Rolland says that roles in the Hamburg opera were sung by students, artisans, shoemakers, tailors, fruit merchants, and girls of dubious virtue. At least the Hamburgers were spared professional opera singers.

Handel arrived. It was here that Handel met his friend Mattheson. Mattheson said of his new acquaintance that he couldn't write a decent melody and couldn't count to five. Both of these criticisms may have been justified. Zachacow couldn't write a good melody either so Handel had come by this lack honestly, and most musicians can't count to three, much less five. The friendship with Mattheson became so intense it resulted in a duel, and Handel's life was saved because he had the foresight to wear a jacket with large metal buttons which parried one of the sword thrusts of his opponent. While he was living in Hamburg, Handel journeyed to Luebeck to investigate becoming Boxtahund's successor. One part of the deal was that to get the job the incumbent had to marry the old composer's old daughter. Handel took one look at her and left on the next coach. So did several hundred other aspirants to the position.

While at Hamburg Handel wrote his first two operas: *Der in Krohnen erlangte Gluecks-Wechsel* and *Die durch Blut und Mord erlangte Liebe.* He may have known something about writing good operas, but he certainly had trouble thinking up catchy titles for them. The operas failed because of a strike by the sign painters.

Handel now decided to leave Germany and travel to Italy where all the real nonsense of opera was going on. First he went to Venice, where the first public opera house had opened as early as 1637. There were now seven opera houses, but none of them would produce operas with names similar to those above. Handel left in an irate mood for Rome. Here he spent his most productive Italian years, and came into contact with a host of helpful composers: Alessandro and Dominico Scarlatti, Corelli, Vivaldi, Pasquini, Steffani, and the two Vermicelli brothers, Fettuccini and Manicotti. Most of his time Handel spent in copying works by these composers for use in future borrowings, plagiarisms, or just plain thefts.

Soon Handel was back in Germany where he obtained an appointment as musician to the Elector of Hanover. Handel, however, could see no future in writing dull Lutheran church music when he could write degenerate Italian opera. He absented himself, went to England, and never returned. In London Handel and his music became an immediate rage. In the first place, he was a foreigner and that gave him a tremendous advantage. In the second place, he was a German who could write in the Italian style. All this was too much for the English to fathom and they applauded vehemently. Handel had by this time settled on shorter titles such as *Rinaldo* and *Il pastor fido* (The Faithful Shepherd, Fido). Although the English could not understand the operas, they could remember the titles.

Handel was just getting settled toward making his first million pounds when his patroness,

Queen Anne, had the insensitivity to die. And who should be made King of England but Handel's *ersazt* patron, the Elector of Hanover from whom the composer had earlier fled. In order to mend fences, or perhaps to escape the gallows for treason, Handel wrote two works for the king's entertainment, *The Royal Firecracker Musick* and *The Wateringtroughmusick,* which was played when the king rested his horses.

Handel now settled into the life of an English businessman in music. We are told he composed with exceeding rapidity, but perhaps we should say he copied with exceeding rapidity. Everyone else's music had a habit of cropping up unannounced in Handel's works. Handel took all the credit and what little blame there was for these thefts. When a true Italian composer, Bononcini, appeared on the scene, Handel was horrified for fear that his sources would be revealed. Bononcini did nothing of the kind. Instead he stole entire opera scenes from Handel. There is no honor amongst thieves.

Toward the end of his life, Handel lost favor with the mercurial English opera audiences. Hence he turned his attention to oratorio, a form that the English had hardly considered until Handel convinced them that it was just like opera and could be performed during Lent. Handel's most famous work is, of course, *Messiah,* which is not to be confused with *The Messiah,* which is something else indeed. We know that everyone now stands for the famous Hallelujah chorus at the end of Act II. During the first performance, the Prince of Wales, who was by this time tired and bored, stood. Everybody else who was tired and bored also stood and the habit caught on. By the end of Act II of most modern performances of *Messiah,* anyone with good taste and judgment should be tired and bored. In fact, he should leave.

The End of the Broque

From the turn of the eighteenth century onward, composers in one country after another were breaking out of the Broque. Although no one told Handel when he was there, the Italians had all gotten out by 1700. The French claimed they had never been Broque at all but had been *classique* all along. The English did what the Italians and French suggested so their opinion didn't count anyway. Only the Germans and particularly J. S. Bach got stuck in the Broque until midcentury. Bach's sons, however, had already had enough. P.D.Q., as usual, had had too much. They all conspired to put the old man to rest with a performance of his famous cantatata, *Ich habe genug* (I've had a Hellev' enough). The Broque was finally broken; all passions ceased; and men turned to their least reliable faculty, reason for their sustenance.

Everyone in the Broque had been so serious that composers had to have a resting period before they could get going again. As a result, for about twenty years there was a mini-period in which everyone wrote what we might call banana split music (i.e. music based on monkey food, ice cream, excess carbohydrates, chocolate syrup, and whipping cream). In such a musical environment, hardly a thing of consequence could be composed, and so we will leave the Rocoocoo Period without further to-do.[14]

[14] Some composers of the period resented being called "Rocoocoo" and preferred to be called "pre-Classic." The subtle difference between the two is merely the difference between banana splits and chocolate ice cream sundaes topped with chopped bananas.

Chapter V
Music in the Classic Period or Why You Shouldn't Say You Like Classical Music if What You Mean is the Beatles

One of the strangest notions people have is that only one facet of human personality is trustworthy at any one time. The Broque trusted the validity of human passions for a century and a half before it was discovered that passions could lead man possibly to good, but more often to evil. One would have thought that fact would have been obvious with the first *auto de fe* of the Inquisition or the first sack of a German village during the Thirty Years War.[1] But then, people do learn slowly. In any event, the passion for passion went out of fashion, and a fashion for reason became reasonable. Again, one wonders why perceptive thinkers had not long ago learned that it is most unreasonable to expect even reasonable men to act reasonably for a reasonable amount of time, much less permanently.

Whenever Western man has championed reason, he has had a peculiar inclination to attribute it to the Greeks.[2] Just why the Greeks should have been made such paragons of reason has never been made clear, but it has something to do with Plato and a cave. Now, as everyone knows, the Greeks were classic. Even they knew they were classic, since they used Doric columns. Nothing is more classic than that. Since the late 18th century was no longer Broque, it had to be something; and since it stressed reason, it might as well be classic. That is where a real problem in the history of music begins.

In the name of reason, we must attempt to clarify. If one says he likes classical music, he doesn't necessarily mean he likes the music of Mozart, Haydn, or Beethoven. He may hate the music of all the principal classic composers, who aren't all the principal classical composers, and still like classical music. The term *classical* refers both to music that is classical and not classical, all at the same time; but it does not refer to the music of the classical Greeks, which isn't classical at

[1] Or for that matter, in any dorm room of any American college after midnight on Saturday evening.

[2] Not the Greeks who run shipping lines but the earlier ones that fought The Peloponnesian War and had gods who slept around with earthly or earthy maidens.

all, but is really the only classical music which doesn't exist. Somehow all good music has become classical, although it isn't; but not all classical music is good, although it should be. These days, any music which survives more than thirty days in the top forty is classical, moreso, it seems, than the *Jupiter Symphony* of Mozart.[3]

It was, of course, much more difficult for musicians to make their music sound classical, than for architects to make their buildings look classical. All the latter had to do was to watch their symmetry[4] and to use Doric columns. Since the Greeks had had the good sense to have all their music lost for posterity, there was nothing similar for musicians of the eighteenth century to copy. The better, and hence more classical, musical minds of the day did take some reasonable steps. In the first place, they decided that music should be enjoyed more and cried over less. Even when setting such a text as "Lord, have mercy," the classical composer uses such verve that no one, including the Good Lord, can take the sentiment more seriously than he ought. In the second place, these composers decided music should have melodies, such as "Twinkle, Twinkle, Little Star," that everyone could remember and could sing. No serious composer had ever thought about writing such a melody before but instead left such trifles to folk musicians. Finally, these composers decided that it was a lot more fun to make music with a fiddle than with a castrato. As a result, more music was now written which stressed instruments than stressed sexually handicapped males. The spirit of everything was freer, happier, and more democratic.[5]

The Symphony

The heart of the new classical style is to be found in orchestral music in the medium of the symphony. The reader will remember that the overtures to Broque operas constituted their most interesting music. When composers simply did away with the operas and left the overtures, the symphony was born. A symphony, then, can be defined as an opera with everything after the overture omitted. One can easily see how this procedure was infinitely more reasonable. It was easy to write lots of overtures (or symphonies as they were now called), if one didn't have to write the operas that went with them. Not only that, but symphonies were cheaper to produce, since one didn't have to pay for singers, stage directors, designers, or the bribes to attract an audience.[6]

[3] If you understand all of this, dear reader, your reason is more classical than that of the author.

[4] Symmetry is important in classicism.

[5] At least democratic from the viewpoint of such people as the Count of Esterhazy.

[6] The demise of opera left the *castrati* at a double loss.

An out-of-fashion castrato updates his skills by learning to play the violin.

It has been asserted that Haydn was the father of the symphony. Actually, the symphony had reached early childhood when he came on the scene. One figure in its early history is Johann Stammeritz, who developed an orchestra at Mannheim which was famous throughout Europe. Until Stammeritz' time it had not occurred to anyone that orchestras needed discipline. Earlier string players had each bowed away as he saw fit without any two agreeing upon anything. Such a style was appropriate to the grossness of the Broque concerto, but inappropriate to the new symphony. The latter form was German (i.e. Prussian), and it demanded the skill of a general and his musical troops. Since Stammeritz' ideal was Frederick the Great, he, Stammeritz, was a perfect candidate for generalissimo in music. In the 18th century, if you couldn't find a battle to watch, you could go hear the Mannheim orchestra. The effect was similar.

Stammeritz and his cohorts also invented a number of technical devices important in the further history of classic style. The first and most important was musical dynamics, the louds and softs of music. No one had ever paid much attention to dynamics,[7] and composers rarely wrote any markings in their scores to hint at what they might have wanted. The Mannheim School,[8] however, invented the crescendo. The string players would begin softly, bowing rapid sixteenth notes in a highly disciplined fashion. They would get louder and louder until the hall seemed to explode with what became known as the Mannheim steamroller.[9] Everyone got out of the way as fast as possible. Stammeritz also invented a new type of theme which began low on the violin and lept rapidly upwards through the notes of the common chord. This new type of theme was called the Mannheim rocket. Whenever a player in the orchestra became undisciplined (i.e. whenever he laughed at the conductor), Stammeritz would have him impaled on a rocket theme and hurled right into the audience. Since there was no Federation of Musicians to protect inept orchestral players, the poor man soon found himself applying for a post at some obscure court in the Polish provinces.

The famous English traveler Charles Burney, who wrote more than he should have about the musical performances he heard, was impressed by the Mannheim string playing. He, however, also said the wind instruments played out of tune and that the beds in the local Holiday Inn

[7] For that matter, many players today don't pay too much attention to dynamics. They want to play loud all the time.

[8] Not the Mannheim Elementary School but the composers at Mannheim who organized themselves into a school which didn't teach any pupils but was convenient for musicologists.

[9] Luckily James Watt had recently invented the steam engine and a name could, then, be provided for this new technique.

A musician being shot out on a Mannheim rocket.

were too soft. Englishmen always are complaining about something, particularly when they are away from England where they should complain about everything.

The Problem of Form

One very important aspect of all classical music, and the symphony is no exception, is the formal order of its various parts. The classical mind wanted everything filed in the proper drawer, and this need was felt in music as clearly as anywhere else. Most classical compositions, symphonies, sonatas, and chamber music, are made up of individual pieces each called a movement. Just where each is moving is not very clear. Perhaps the first movement moves to the second, the second to the third, and the third to the finale, which doesn't move anywhere, since it is final. Early classical composers experimented with pieces which had as few as a single movement, which didn't move at all, and as many as six movements which moved too much. Finally, at the Congress of Vienna, all composers agreed that four was the proper compromise.

If you were writing a proper symphony, if you knew what you were doing as some did not, the first movement was fast and in sonata-allegro form. Unfortunately, we must return to this later. The second movement had to be slow and pathetic enough to get people to cry themselves to sleep. The third movement was a courtly dance, the minuet, so that everyone could wake up. Beethoven replaced this minuet with a scherzo, or joke. Just what the joke was he didn't explain. Beethoven was German, and Germans are noted for their limited sense of humor. The finale, which was always a relief to everyone, was often in rondo or round-about form. We will discuss this, too, presently.

The sonata-allegro form was the most important of all the formal orders of musical classicism. The form was not only used in sonatas but also in symphonies, concertos, chamber music, and even opera arias. Also it occurs in movements which were not fast (i.e. allegros). Just why the form should have been called what it was is not clear. Perhaps symphonic-adagio form would have been as good. A classical composer first had to study the outlines of a given form as they were contained in the many form and analysis textbook on the shelves of his library. When he understood all the parts thoroughly, he had merely to fill in the form much as one fills in a form for the Internal Revenue Service. The whole matter was only a bit less confusing.

Sonata-allegro forms have three sections which parallel the three periods of a composer's life. These sections are the exposition, in which all the themes come out of the closet; the development, where they are subjected to as much scrutiny as the composer can imagine; and finally the retread. The retread was always the easiest to write, since all the composer had to do was to go back to the exposition and copy it all over again.

The exposition, and hence the retread, should contain at least two good themes. The first theme was in the home key to get everything completely settled, but the second theme was in a contrasting key. Thinking of one good theme was more than most composers could manage; thinking of two was out of the question; and changing from one key to another was a matter best left to Mozart. Not everyone could manage the form expertly, no matter how seriously he tried.[10] Some composers further confused sonata-allegro form by opening it with a slow introduction which they wrote to pass the time until two good themes could present themselves. The form was often ended by an extended coda, in which all the violins could fiddle away faster and faster, all the brass players could blow harder and harder, the tympany player could play bong-bong-bong-bong to his heart's content, and the conductor could show off before the audience by making wild flourishes.[11]

The rondo or round-about form is easiest explained by an analogy to a person lost in the woods. He keeps wandering and wandering, but every so often keeps returning to his starting point. The rondo is just like this. The composer begins with a good first theme but soon begins to wander from it. For want of anything better, he returns to it, wanders some more, returns to the theme, and so forth until he gets tired and stops to await rescue. The form is easy to write since the composer must think of only one good theme and getting lost is second nature to most composers.

Another form used by the classicists is the theme and perpetual variation. Classical composers usually chose themes which were tunes everyone knew, such as "God Save the King" or "My County 'tis of Thee" depending upon which side of the Atlantic one happened to be. Hearing this tune once or even twice may inspire patriotism, but when Beethoven wrote thirty-two variations on it, the result was something else again. The classical variation is based on the notion that if eighth-note motion is good, sixteenth is better, and thirty-second note motion the best of

[10] The idea of development was so foreign to some composers that they merely omitted the section altogether. Beethoven, however, who from the beginning to the end of his life was always developing, made the most out of this section.

[11] Beethoven often chose to end his symphonies with twenty-five identical chords. Orchestral players always hope the conductor will conduct only twenty-four of these and embarrass himself. This is, however, one of the few places conductors routinely count.

all. The more notes on the page the better the variation. The idea is to play faster and faster until the hands of the performer are aching and the ears of the audience are aching too. Other forms used by the classicists are two-part form, which has only one part repeated twice, and three-part form, which has only two parts, but the first is repeated.

The Concerto

Almost as important as the symphony to classic composers was the solo concerto, generally for piano and orchestra, less frequently for violin and orchestra, but never for bagpipe and orchestra. The new sense of freedom which the late 18th century political philosophers had championed had given rise to a new kind of performer who felt that he was better than anyone else and set out to prove it in public performance. This new virtuoso[12] was convinced that he alone could be more impressive than an entire orchestra. The classical concerto is no more than an attempt to fight this out in public.

Concerti[13] generally have three movements: fast-slow-fast, and they lack the minuet of the symphony. Virtuosi could see no way they could show off playing something as silly as a minuet. One element in the concerto, however, must be mentioned, and that is the cadenza. Near the end of the first movement, and near the ends of the other two if the virtuoso got his way, a chord was held by the orchestra, and this was the signal for the virtuoso to show off without further encumbrances. Since this could take a very long time, the orchestral players could take a nap, the conductor could study the score of the next composition, and members of the audience could excuse themselves to "powder their noses." Eventually even the virtuoso got tired of showing off, so he, the conductor, and the orchestral launched into the coda, hopefully all at the same time. Some composers decided it was best to write out cadenzas so that virtuosi wouldn't be tempted to be too wild. These cadenzas were universally ignored by everyone except musicologists who enjoy finding them.[14]

[12] This word is formed on the same stem which gives us the word "virtuous." A virtuous virtuoso, however, is a contradiction in terms.

[13] Same as "concertos" but it sounds more learned.

[14] They serve as the substance for excellent short articles for the few musicologists who have any interest in writing short articles.

The Piano Sonata

If a virtuoso pianist couldn't find an orchestra when he was ready to perform, he had to settle for a sonata. The sonata is much like the concerto with the orchestra removed. The sonata emphasized the individual performer as much as was possible, since he was the only one playing. Indeed it was the perfect vehicle for the *Strum und Drang* (Ranting and Raving) side of classical expression. Since an element of the classical creed was the importance of the individual, and since the virtuoso was wont to rant and rave more than the average man, it is not surprising that the sonata, in which the performer was free unto himself, became the medium for the *Strum und Drang*. Ripping in scales and arpeggios up and down the keyboard, playing bombastic and dissonant chords, storming in octaves, and stressing the pathetic were all part of the vocabulary. Much of this was less than reasonable, but, as I said, reason can only be temporary.

The piano, piano-forte, or forte-piano[15] had by now displaced the harpsichord. The new instrument, which in English we should really call the soft-loud or loud-soft, could obviously play soft and loud, and since dynamics had just been discovered that was an advantage. Everyone, whether musical or not, wanted to play the piano, and this is what gave rise to the piano teacher and the concomitant curse, the teaching piece. Even Beethoven gave in to the temptation to write such pieces and gave the world his famous *Fuer Elise*. Most piano students wish Elise had thrown the thing away. During the next century the piano got bigger and bigger and louder and louder, and the way to make of it a sensitive musical instrument became stonier and stonier.

Franz Joseph Haydn

Franz Joseph Haydn was born in 1732. If you want to live to be seventy-seven and you want to die in 1809, there is simply no better year to be born than 1732, and that is just what happened. Although Haydn did have parents, he had no origins. Everyone was always trying to account for Haydn's unusual musical gifts except Haydn who was trying to make the most of what he had. Haydn's parents loved him so much they sent him away permanently when he was five-and-a-half. At that age he was taken from his native village to the city of Hainburg. There he lived with the town schoolmaster and musician whose name was Franck. The young boy later complained that Frau Franck wouldn't let him take a bath or wouldn't give him clean clothes. Most six year olds would be in ecstasy over such a situation, but, as we will find, Haydn was

[15] But never the forte, despite the way many performers insist on playing the instrument.

meticulous. Herr Franck didn't seem to be able to teach the young boy too much, so he sent him to Vienna to study under Georg Reutter at the Church of Saint Stephen. Reutter didn't seem to be able to teach Haydn much either, except how to get into trouble. About this time, Haydn's life was made even worse by the arrival at Saint Stephen of his younger and more precocious brother, Michael, who carried a red apple in his hand for Kapelmeister Reutter. Nothing is more obnoxious than a bright younger brother.

Reutter did appreciate Franz Joseph's lovely soprano voice, but as he neared his twelfth year the inevitable began to happen. The Queen, Maria Theresa, complained of the cracking of the lead at mass on Sunday morning, and Haydn had had it or lost it as the case might be. Reutter approached his choirboy with a proposition: i.e. a means by which his luscious voice could be preserved at the cost of something else. Haydn's father, who had not been seen for seven years, heard of this proposition and snatched his son from the surgeon's knife. Errant fathers who appear at the right moment are certainly better than those who don't appear at all. Reutter dismissed the young Haydn and dumped him penniless on the Vienna streets.

Thus began Haydn's garret period. It is always good for a composer to have a garret or poverty period; it steels them for what lies ahead: public acceptance. Haydn was lucky enough to find a garret right above the apartment of the famous poet and librettist, Metastasio. It was not long before Haydn was giving lessons to Metastasio's good-looking daughter. Thus began a pattern which was to last throughout the composer's long life. He always chose, if he could, the daughters or wives of persons of note to be his pupils. It may also be noted that he wrote passionate notes to those daughters and wives of persons of note for the remainder of his noted life. Metastasio was so pleased with Haydn's teaching of his daughter[16] that he introduced the young musician to the composer Porpora, who gave Haydn a job of accompanying and shining shoes. One of Porpora's acquaintances was the Countess Thun, who soon was receiving her instruction. The Countess was forty-five, but nonetheless Haydn had something to teach her. She probably had something to teach him also. The Countess introduced Haydn to Count Morzin who introduced him to the Esterhazy family. From that time on, Hadyn had it made.

It was Count Paul Esterhazy who hired Haydn, but he doesn't count because he died within a year. It was Prince Nicolas who was really Haydn's patron. Nicolas loved music and played an obscure musical instrument called the baryton, for which, for reasons not too clear, Haydn

[16] There is no record that Metastasio actually attended the lessons.

immediately acquired a love. We have the contract in which Haydn's duties are spelled out. Haydn's name is spelled out also, each time incorrectly. Perhaps the Esterhazy family thought that if no one could spell its name correctly, the Esterhazys were entitled to misspell everyone else's. The contract also specifies that Haydn was to "instruct the females" of the family. It seems his skill in this was already infamous.

Nicolas already had a perfectly good palace outside of Vienna at a place called Eisenstadt. Everyone but Nicolas was happy, but he thought he needed another in the middle of a swamp. So, then, he picked the least likely site in all his vast holdings and had the colossal palace of Esterhaza[17] constructed. Everyone moved there and hated it, despite the fact that it had two hundred and sixty-two guest rooms in which the malaria victims could recover. For the next thirty years Haydn had a calm life of producing symphonies, rehearsing the orchestra, instructing the females, and avoiding his wife, whom he had married in one of his few fits of limited reason.[18]

The only thing Haydn liked more than instructing females was writing symphonies, all one hundred four of them (symphonies, that is).[19] As I have said, everyone but Nicolas, the only one who counted anyway, hated Esterhaza. Everyone but the Prince was in a rush to get back to Vienna. Once when Nicolas refused to leave when he said he would, Haydn wrote a symphony in which each of the musicians rose, extinguished his candle, and left with instrument and music in hand. The Prince got the message of the Farewell Symphony, and the court left for Vienna the next day. However, the Prince told Haydn he could take a joke one time, but if there were a second farewell symphony, Haydn could expect to dedicate it to his own farewell.

Haydn was in charge of hiring the finest musicians money could buy. One whom he hired was an aged, decrepit violinist who couldn't play but who had a beautiful, young brunette for a wife. Haydn decided she needed instruction, which he cheerfully provided for the next twenty years. Luigia Polzelli learned slowly, or else Haydn dragged out the lessons in hopes there was something else he could think of to teach her.

[17] The Prince was not too original in thinking up names for his palaces. *Esterhaza* rivaled Versailles in splendor. That was also built in a swamp.

[18] It seems he failed to teach her anything. In fact he avoided lessons with her.

[19] Haydn wrote one hundred four symphonies, Mozart wrote forty-one, Beethoven nine, Brahms four, and Franck only one. It seems that symphonic composers got lazier and lazier as time went on.

In 1790 Prince Nicolas died, and the tranquility which Haydn had enjoyed was broken. The new prince had better sense than to like music. He fired the orchestra and he pensioned Haydn. The composer left the mire of Esterhaza and traveled to London, where he exchanged the relationship with Prince Nicolas for one with the Prince of Wales. We know how great Haydn's acclaim was in England, because the composer wrote detailed letters to a Viennese pupil, Marienne Genziger, whom he had been instructing when Luigia wasn't around. Haydn continued his pedagogical activity in London. His new pupil was a Mrs. Schroeter whom Haydn described to Marienne as very ugly and approaching seventy. Actually, she was very pretty, approaching thirty, and very rich. Haydn, as we have said, chose his pupils carefully. Hadyn cut his journey short when Luigia wrote she was on her way to England for some instruction of her own.

On his second trip to England, Haydn was introduced to their Highnesses, the King and Queen. The Queen, who took a liking to the composer, although she appears never to have taken any instruction from him, urged Haydn to remain permanently in England. He declined and gave for his reason that his wife would object. Since she had been objecting to everything Haydn had done since their marriage began, it is difficult to see what was particularly unusual. In any event, the Queen gave Haydn a parrot which he sold for 1400 florins when he returned to Vienna. Just why a parrot would bring such a price, even if it did come from The Queen of England, no one seems to know.

In the last years of his life, Haydn turned to oratorio. Someone had given him a Bible and suggested he read it in search of a subject. The composer, who hated reading, got no further than the opening of Genesis, and so chose the subject of "The Creation" for his first work of this type. About this time, Haydn was approached by the young Beethoven for instruction. This seems to have ended Haydn's pedagogical career. Haydn, who was much loved by everyone—pupil or not, died in honor. The following verse sums it all up:

Papa Haydn's dead and gone,
But his memory lingers on,
When his mood was one of bliss,
He found another countess to kiss.

Wolfgang Amadeus Mozart

There is not too much to joke about in the life of Wolfgang Amadeus Mozart, and it is probably for that reason that he became the all-time master of opera buffa. Even the comedy in opera is more amusing than his life. In the first place, poor Wolfgang was born a prodigy, and nothing can be more depressing to a young lad than that. There was no chance for little league baseball, cub scouts, or annoying your older sister, particularly if you had to play duets with her to amuse the aristocracy. Everywhere the young Mozarts played, they amused the aristocracy. They were amused, but rarely paid well for the privilege.[20] In the second place, Mozart's father Leopold was a musician and a writer of books, and one can hardly conjure up a person with more threatening characteristics. Leopold so threatened his patron, The Archbishop of Salzburg, that the Archbishop kept him playing second violin for life. Leopold protested that he should be made *Kapelmeister* since he had attended to The Archbishop's business so diligently. Actually Leopold had been largely absent for the preceding decade.

Leopold taught the young Wolfgang everything he knew, which was about equal to what Wolfgang knew when he was six years old. The one thing he didn't seem to teach Wolfgang was the value of the dollar, which, since it was the eighteenth century, still had some value. Wolfgang was always thinking up new schemes to get rich in music fast. Leopold well knew one didn't get rich in music, fast or slow. Leopold also introduced his son to everyone. If Leopold had never met a particular nobleman, it did not deter him in the least. A typical conversation went like this: "Good evening, Your Grace So-and-So. I am Leopold Mozart, the father of the world's greatest musical genius (Leopold was known for his honesty). I've also written a book about how to play the violin, which you really should read. Wouldn't you like me to send twenty copies for Your Grace's fine library? I'll send the invoice to your secretary. Also, my son and his sister are available for a concert at your palace next Saturday. The fee is only six hundred florins, and Wolfgang will write a little minuet especially for the occasion. You do know His Majesty, King So-and-So? Would you introduce me? I know he too would like to read my book and hear my son." One can certainly see how tiring this kind of thing could be to a lad of seven, no matter how great a genius he might have been. Wolfgang even played for Marie Antoinette, who said, "Let him eat cake." Leopold would have been happier with six hundred *louis d'or*.

Since all the normal activities for a young boy were denied Mozart, who must have hated bouncing around the countryside in unairconditioned coaches hunting for new nobility to be milked, the young boy wrote letters, hundreds of them to anyone who would write back. Some of

[20] Queen Victoria had not yet set the tone "We are not amused" for European royalty.

the letters, particularly ones to a kissing cousin, are full of four letter words and suggestive passages. It is lucky Mozart didn't choose pornographic literature as a career. He had far less genius for it than he had for music. On the other hand, these letters have given musicologists something to snicker at, and anything that can make those people laugh has got to be to the good.

Leopold, who couldn't impress The Archbishop much himself, decided to try to impress The Archbishop with Wolfgang. The Archbishop replied he was not impressed, at least not impressed enough to offer the young genius a living wage. In any case, The Archbishop already had Haydn's brother, Michael, in his employ and that composer could turn out all the banal music which Salzburg could use. Wolfgang told The Archbishop to shove it, and The Archbishop shoved Mozart right out of Salzburg. About this time, Mozart married his beloved Constanza, whose constancy one could hardly question but whose good sense one could. About all the good young Constanza did for the composer was to give him another address to which he could write letters. Leopold was horrified at all of this.

Mozart now had no job, a wife, complete with mother-in-law, who was no help either. He did the best thing he knew. He started going from one royal court to another, insulting its prince, and asking for a job. Mozart never understood that it was a rare nobleman who could understand the difference between one musician and another. It was even a rarer nobleman who would tolerate the conduct of a one-time child prodigy, be he genius or not. If there were ever anyone who needed the aid of a first class career planning office, Mozart certainly did.

Life was grim, so Mozart turned to opera. Why he should have thought that would help his situation God only knows, but it certainly helped opera. Only the world's greatest musical genius could make anything out of that, and he did. In the first place, Mozart decided it would be better to portray real people in his operas, and not gods and goddesses. This idea was revolutionary enough. In the second place, he decided that the aristocracy, which paid for the operas, would be willing to serve as the laughing stock in his libretti. This idea was really revolutionary, so revolutionary that some of Mozart's operas were banned. Finally, Mozart decided that when the finale of an opera finally arrived, it would be good to have some good music so that everyone could agree the work was finally a success. He had all the principal characters sing, all at the same time, about anything which they happened to be thinking at the moment. It was such confusion that no one could understand any of the words. But . . ., you were forced to listen to the music, and that music was by Mozart. Only Mozart could write a Mozartian finale, but then Mozart was the only one foolhardy enough to try.

A musicologist reads a Mozart letter.

There is a legend that the rival composer, Salieri, tried to poison Mozart out of jealousy for his operatic successes. What successes? Salieri had all the successes. Mozart should have poisoned him. Salieri did come to Mozart's funeral. Hardly anyone else but Constanza did.

One ray of light in Mozart's last years was his friendship with Haydn. "Dear Papa" realized that here was one person whom he didn't have to instruct. Indeed, for once in his long life, there was finally one person who could instruct Franz Joseph. Mozart also met the young Beethoven. Mozart said, "He will make a noise in the world." Probably what Mozart meant was that Beethoven would make too much noise in the world, and that is what happened.

Ludwig van Beethoven

The classical tradition so carefully built up by Mozart and Haydn passed to the shoulders of a provincial musician from the wrong side of Germany, who didn't even know how to powder his wig properly. Ludwig[21] van[22] Beethoven was born in Bonn instead of Vienna, which would have been more appropriate. His father was the town drunk, and his mother was a chambermaid in the Elector's household. Hardly had the young Ludwig learned about the birds and the bees, than he was saying that momma was more than a chambermaid in the Elector's bedroom, and that he, Beethoven, deserved the "van" in his name. For one whose entire life was devoted to a hatred of the nobility, Beethoven, more than any other composer, tried to assert his right to its privileges. He said that nobility did not spring from birth, although he tried his best to doctor up his own. Instead, nobility sprang from the soul. It was a nice idea, and everyone but the nobility wholeheartedly agreed.

Despite the fact that Beethoven loved Bonn and liked to look at the Rhine, which is easy to do there since it flows right by the city, he wanted to get where the action was. Although the Elector wouldn't acknowledge Beethoven as his son, he paid for his trip to Vienna; thereby he avoided a lawsuit. Beethoven hoped to study composition with Mozart, but before the lessons could be arranged, poor Mozart was dead. The only thing timely about Mozart's death was that he escaped having to teach the young ruffian. They would have gotten on as well as water mixes with oil.

Haydn, however, was still alive and still willing to instruct anyone who could pay the fee.

[21] Which is the same as Louis only more colorful.
[22] Which, despite Beethoven's efforts, didn't mean a thing.

Beethoven said he wanted to study counterpoint, and Haydn said he had never cared much for the subject. He would be willing, he said, to teach Beethoven about symphonic development. Since Beethoven already had some ideas about that subject, he said, "No thank you," and left. Beethoven had a habit of running out on all the right people. The nobility within his soul kept acting up like indigestion. Beethoven got a hack to teach him counterpoint. Just what Beethoven taught the hack is not recorded.

Beethoven hit the Viennese social scene like a bombshell.[23] In carrying boorishness to an art form, Beethoven established for the first time the concept of the erratic musical artist, a concept which, from that day to this, some of the wealthy have been willing to buy. Since Beethoven could not possibly allow his nobility of soul to be burdened by a patron, he had several of them at the same time. Each vied with the others to give the composer free room and board and be insulted in the process. Beethoven had certain standards in selecting his patrons. First of all, they naturally had to have money. Each had to have the capacity to be insulted for pay. A pretty sixteen year old daughter for Beethoven to fall in love with helped immensely. Finally the strange Beethoven required his prospective patron to have a name similar to those found in the backfield of the Pittsburgh Steelers. Lichnowsky, Lobkowitz, Oulibicheff, Liechstenstein, and Galitsin all qualified.

All of this Beethoven carried off without having composed anything of particular consequence. Everytime Beethoven was asked to play, he improvised, and for several years none of his patrons discovered he had hardly put a note on paper. When they found out, he got to work. It was lucky this came when it did, for the composer's first creative period was coming to an end, and he hadn't created too much. He got to work on his first symphony, which everyone said sounded like Haydn. Hadyn didn't agree. He said it sounded like the work of a student composer who didn't show up for lessons.

Beethoven's second creative period began with the growing awareness that he was gradually becoming deaf. Beethoven's enemies all said that the composer's music was driving everyone else deaf; why shouldn't he suffer the same fate. One queer aspect of the composer's malady was its selective nature. Beethoven could always hear his admirers praise his works, but he could never hear a word his critics said. Beethoven consulted one physician after another in hopes of finding a cure for his condition. Finally, he exclaimed that what he needed was less a cure for his

[23] Real bombshells hit the Viennese social scene a few years later when Napoleon arrived.

deafness than a cure for what the doctors had done trying to correct it. It was his deafness which gave rise to the famous document, the so-called Heiligenstadt Testament. Beethoven addressed the text, in which he bemoans the prospects of his future life, to his two brothers, one whose name he seems to have forgotten. If you had brothers similar to those Beethoven had, you would promptly forget their names, if you could.

Beethoven saw that posterity would remember him best for his symphonies so he got to work on them as seriously as he could. It was in this third symphony[24] the so-called Eroica, in which he really hit his stride. The symphony was long, arduous, and profound, and the audience at its first performance found it long, arduous, and confusing. One critic said that the symphony contained moments of great originality, but that the work, as a whole, was incoherent. He recommended that Beethoven study the symphonies of Mozart, Haydn, and Eberl. Beethoven was forced to consult the Vienna telephone directory in order to locate Eberl, who was the owner of a local pawn shop and a friend of the critic.

This symphony, as everyone knows, was originally dedicated to Napoleon, whom Beethoven regarded as a champion of liberty. Beethoven, of course, tore the title page from the work when he learned that Napoleon had had himself made emperor. The composer was opposed to anyone but himself becoming noble by the back door. A lesser known fact is that Beethoven altered the nature of the second movement so that it became a funeral march. He proclaimed the symphony would bury Napoleon, not praise him.

Perhaps the best known moment in the symphony is the premature appearance of the main theme directly before the true retread of the first movement. Beethoven had, by mistake, left two measures out of the horn part. When the horn player came in, as his score directed him, he was soundly rebuked by the conductor for improper counting. Beethoven, who was present, was furious. "I wrote it, and that is the way it should be," he exclaimed. So it has been to this day. Those with nobility in their souls do not make mistakes.

After having tossed off another little pleasantry, the fourth symphony,[25] he set himself to the task of writing the most famous piece of orchestral music of all time. As we can imagine, this turned out to be the fifth symphony. In order to accomplish a task of this magnitude, the

[24] The second symphony doesn't count. It was a little thing the composer dashed off on the spur of the moment during one of his love affairs.

[25] Beethoven had a thing against even numbers. He thought they should be played down.

Beethoven exercises his option of rejecting a patron.

composer needed a theme everyone could recognize. He realized that everyone would recognize the Morse code for "vee," which could stand for victory, so he chose the theme of three dots and a dash. You will remember that Churchill was pleased.

One characteristic of Beethoven's personality was that he was always developing. He developed new patrons, new levels of rudeness, new places to live,[26] new heroes, new bank accounts, new law suits, but most of all he developed the development sections of symphonies. In his development sections, Beethoven develops motives in what is known as motivic development. A tiny bit of music material (i.e. the motive), such as "dot, dot, dot, dash" is developed until it has become, three hundred measures later, simply "dot, dot, dot, dash"; only you have heard it several thousand times. The fifth symphony is a model for such development. Not only was Beethoven able to develop development sections. He also developed the coda. The coda is a tailpiece of a musical composition. Beethoven developed his codas until they wagged the rest of his compositions.

The sixth symphony, the so-called Pastoral, contains the sounds of rustling brooks, thunder, and bird calls. It proves that Beethoven had been using his deficient hearing during his walks in the Vienna woods. No one ever says much about the seventh symphony except that it is magnificent and needs a name. Beethoven tossed off the little eighth symphony in a matter of weeks during the summer of 1812, which like so many summers didn't last but a matter of weeks. Unfortunately everyone has been tossing it off ever since, despite the fact that it is really very lovely. Many people had criticized Beethoven for writing symphonies which were so long. Now he had written a short symphony, and his critics said it was too short. The work of critics is to criticize, and we cannot criticize them for what they do best, criticism.

Before we turn to Beethoven's last period and his last symphony, we should mention one of the many problems of his personal life, his nephew Karl, the son of his brother of the same name and similar problems. At his brother's death, Beethoven engaged in a law suit to wrest the younger Karl from a mother who had so little sense as to want the boy in the first place. She should have thanked God for her brother-in-law, not sued him. Beethoven demanded that the case be heard in an upper court since he was of noble extraction. The upper court said that anyone so insane as to want this Karl should be heard in magistrates court and nowhere else. Beethoven wanted his nephew to go to college, and you can imagine where that would have led.

[26] Beethoven changed residences over sixty times during his life.

Instead Karl attempted suicide and unfortunately failed even in that. Karl summed up the matter well when he declared, "I have become worse because my uncle wanted me to do better." The follies of youth are not limited by historical boundaries.

The problems with Karl and the composer's now near total deafness were compounded by the fact that Beethoven's annuity had been cut in half by inflation. He didn't even have the Democrats to blame. Beethoven became so tired of it all that he proclaimed his third, and naturally last, creative period had begun. He also decided that one unique symphony was appropriate for his last period. Up until now composers had been willing to put up only with instrumentalists in their symphonies. Now Beethoven was willing to risk singers, an entire chorus of them, plus four screaming soloists. As his inspiration he took a beer hall poem which was not worth a *Schilling*. The poem dealt with a strange maiden named Freude who was the daughter of the king of Elysium. It contained funny words such as *Götterfunken* which cannot be translated into English.[27] The chorus sits quietly by for three long movements before the bass gets tired of it all and sings in a loud voice, "No, not these sounds." Finally when the chorus does get to sing, it makes the most of its chance. The sopranos get to hold a high A for fourteen measures, and nothing could please sopranos more. They love to screech, the higher the better.

It was fortunate that the Ninth Symphony was profound music, just as Beethoven said it would be. At the first performance, the audience had to sit through an hour and a half of music before the conductor got around to the symphony, which was itself equally as long. Everyone was ecstatic when he finally could leave. The reason the last movement is called "The Ode to Joy" was only too clear when you finally got to stand up.

With the death of Beethoven,[28] classicism and a number of other things, such as Beethoven's annuity, came to an end. Poor Schubert died the very next year. He had tried to be classic, but he kept writing all those beautiful songs which didn't qualify. Besides, he had left a symphony unfinished, and classic composers certainly wouldn't do anything that unreasonable.

[27] The work is always sung in German so that nobody will laugh.

[28] Twenty thousand persons attended Beethoven's funeral, despite the fact that only six had turned out for Mozart's. Funerals had become more popular in Vienna in the early nineteenth century.

Chapter VI
Music in the Romantic Period
or
Nobody Can Fall in Love Without a Gushy Melody

As we pointed out in the last chapter, human reason is a fragile and temporal commodity, and the age based upon it proved equally fragile and temporal. When faced by the realization that the peasants had no bread to eat, Marie Antoinette applied her sense of reason and suggested that they eat cake. The peasants, who, of course, had no cake either,[1] thought it more reasonable to lop off Marie Antoinette's head along with the heads of a lot of other reasonable, sensible, and wealthy people. Certainly, at the beginning some of this was reasonable; there are always persons who function infinitely more reasonably without their brains than in possession of them. But the guillotine[2] made the process all too easy, very expeditious, and perhaps even a bit enjoyable. As a result, most of the nobility of France, were soon standing in line to take part in the newest fad:[3] decapitation. It all got out of hand, and before reason could intervene, the French Revolution was born.[4] The demise of reason led to Romanticism, and a new artistic age was born.

Romanticism can be defined very simply as looking at the world through rose-colored glasses which are slightly dirty. The prospective such glasses give improves the reality of nearly everything. Thus, a new sense of heightened reality is a basic concomitant of Romanticism. The romantic could, for instance, look at nature and see only bright summer days, crystal lakes, beautiful flowers, and verdant pastures, but his glasses prevented him from seeing such irrelevant natural phenomena as earthquakes, hurricanes, shipwrecks, and world famine. Naturally, everyone ran to his or her[5] optometrist to have another miracle of the Industrial Revolution

[1] The close relationship between the possession of bread and the possession of cake has not yet been thoroughly explored by supply-side economics.

[2] One of the earliest and most successful products of the Industrial Revolution.

[3] The nobility always jumps at the newest thing, be it guillotines or Gucci jeans.

[4] The Industrial Revolution was something else, but just as bloody.

[5] Women were very much into Romanticism.

immediately fitted. Lens grinders worked night and day grinding new glass in just the right tint of vinegared rosé. This color even became a symbol of the Romantic age.[6]

The Romantics were obsessed with history and the past. It was not, however, the history and the past which had actually occurred but that which they saw through their rose-colored glasses. They were particularly fond of knights and castles, armor and lances, medievil cathedrals in ruins, and sagas and lays.[7] Everyone who could afford to do so had his own ruin constructed in the back yard. If you couldn't afford a ruin, you could commission your writer in residence to do a short saga of four thousand pages. You might hire your tinsmith, who should have been engaged in more profitable labor such as the fabrication of furnace ducts, to do you a suit of armor, complete with lance and plume. If you were really poor, you had to make do with searching for flowers in crannied walls. Just what a crannied wall is or just why flowers should choose such an unlikely place to grow is difficult to explain. It was so very much fun to be romantic, particularly if you didn't have to make your own living.[8] Economic historians have never been able to explain how most romantics made their living unless they were engaged in real estate sales of old castles.

There was no way Romanticism could fail to affect music. Even the strong tradition of Mozartean reason could not prevail against it. John Paul[9] said that music was the most romantic of all the arts, because no matter how hard one tried, one could never catch it. Why the romantics should have wanted to chase music when they equally well could have chased women is clear evidence of their almost universal delusion. Schubert had already written a song about an irresponsible father dragging his unwilling son around on a horse in the middle of the night.[10] Even Beethoven had tried an opera in the romantic tradition. That faithful *Fidelio* had fearfully failed three times is good reason to believe Ludwig just couldn't get with it. The problem was that both Schubert and Beethoven were German, and in Germany vestigial remains of reason were still to be found.[11] We must move to France, something Germans rarely like to do, if we are to

[6] It is to be found ad nauseum in every Victorian living room.

[7] Don't misunderstand this word. Be a good student, look it up in the dictionary, and get your mind out of the gutter.

[8] The typical American undergraduate presently maintains this point of view.

[9] Persons whose last names make good first names are always suspect. They can easily swap one for the other, and, in the process, become schizophrenic.

[10] There were then few laws to prevent child abuse which could end in death by overexposure.

[11] In this respect, note the works of Goethe, despite the fact he couldn't spell his name.

understand the deep nature of romantic perversity. In the works of Hector Berlioz[12] we find this carried to musical perfection.

Hector Berlioz

Hector Berlioz was born in southern France and, from the Parisian point of view, could know nothing about music or anything else of consequence. Berlioz had a father who knew the value of a franc, and he decided young Hector should be a physician.[13] Hector, who knew the value of nothing at all but had a father to support him,[14] decided to become a musician. Since Hector could not play any instrument, didn't care to learn, and could not sing either, his decision to become a composer was made by the process of elimination. Hardly had he arrived in Paris, when he proclaimed himself France's most brilliant composer. This really wasn't saying too much since the competition consisted of the one hundred six year old Gretry; Auber, the writer of comic operas; and Meyerbeer, who was German and didn't count anyway. The French didn't know if Berlioz assertion was true or not since during the Revolution they had successfully decapitated everyone who possessed the slightest element of *bon gout*, so they decided to have a riot about the matter.[15] Berlioz' advocates made the most noise, erected the most formidable barriers, unfurled the most flags, and stoned the most gendarmes. They won, and Berlioz was it.

Such a Parisian reception made it necessary for the young composer to produce a masterwork, so Berlioz took up where Beethoven had never thought of leaving off, and produced his *Sympathy Fantastique.* This work became one of the pivotal works of European music.[16] The art has been spinning ever since. The importance of the work lies, to a great degree, in its contribution to program music, an important element of nineteenth century musical tradition. Berlioz had observed that the non-aristocratic audiences of his day fidgeted through most concerts. He concluded that if each concert goer had a piece of paper to play with, particularly one which had printed on it a lurid story, audience behavior would improve. After members of the audience had done their reading, they could doodle on the back of the sheet, make funny hats or paper

[12] Believe me, reader, this was his name.

[13] This was prior to the advent of socialized medicine which put a more accurate premium on the French medical profession.

[14] He may have had some talent also, but that was not nearly as important.

[15] From 1789 to the present, the French will riot about anything more serious than a piece of burned toast.

[16] There is no way the Asians can be blamed for it.

The audience reads Berlioz' new programme notes.

airplanes to sail into the hall, or make spitballs to shoot at the conductor. The result was not as successful as Berlioz had hoped, for he later lamented to his close friends that the program had gotten in the way of his music. He was wrong. Anything which could thwart Berlioz' orchestral style must have had the specific gravity of pig iron.

The story Berlioz wrote for his program was autobiographical, a fact that in itself was justification for the authorities to incarcerate the young fanatic for life. It revolved about his infatuation for a young actress, who drove him to drugs and danced at his funeral. As I have suggested, the romantics could be inspired by the most outrageous nonsense. In order to represent his beloved musically, Berlioz invented a lovely melody.[17] Everytime one thought he had heard the last of the melody, it reappeared much as an unwanted girl friend. Here Berlioz demonstrates the romantic trait of stubbornness, and his *ideé fixe*, or dogged idea, became his musical trademark. The last movement of the sympathy is based on a Gregorian chant played by the trombones and tuba while the beloved theme is screeched six octaves above by the E-flat clarinet. Such unique concern for orchestral timbres[18] became another obsession of Romantic composers. Berlioz decided to write a book about the art of orchestration. All the examples in it were from the works of Berlioz, who, as far as he was concerned, was the only one who knew anything about the orchestra. As far as all other composers were concerned, Berlioz was the only one who understood his book, so that not too much was accomplished. Composers should leave the writing of textbooks to college professors, who need the extra income.

Berlioz was the first of the great romantic composers to prefer huge instrumental and vocal forces. This he derived from his military counterpart, Napoleon, who was a military genius. One of Napoleon's most unique observations was that an army of one million men stood a fair chance of winning a battle against an army of only one hundred thousand. The genius of great military minds had always improved western culture.

Louis Napoleon[19] once greeted Berlioz in this fashion, "Monsieur Berlioz, you are the composer who writes for four hundred musicians." Berlioz replied, "Sir, you have been misinformed. I write for four thousand." Modesty was not the composer's strong suit. Neither was tact, for that matter.

[17] One of the great gifts of romantic composers was their many lovely melodies which they contrived for popular composers of our century to steal.

[18] The same as timbers, only it sounds more learned.

[19] Not the real Napoleon, although he would have liked to have been.

Berlioz' final demise came in opera, a milieu which has provided the demise for many characters, fictional and non-fictional. His opera, *Les Troyens,*[20] was over eight hours long, too long for even the few who love opera. That alone might have been endured, but Berlioz demanded the construction of a horse one hundred and twenty feet high, four hundred feet long, and weighing thirty-eight tons. It crashed through the stage of the Paris Opera and into the infamous Parisian sewers, which were clogged for days by the debris. The result, as well as the stench, was an event that even Berlioz could no longer top.

The Romantic Virtuoso: Frans List and Nicololo Paganinini

To the romantic mind,[21] the individual was everything, and to the romantic musician, he was the personification of everything. We have already encountered the virtuoso and his excesses in classical music, but by the nineteenth century he had grown up and become really dangerous. As the sappling, so the tree; only with the virtuoso, moreso. To become a true romantic virtuoso required considerable training. We have an extant textbook on the subject: *Essai sur l'art das wahre Virtuoso zu machen* (Paris et/und Leipzig, 1825) by the French German scholar Cheval Mastdarm (1821-1826). Here the author outlines the requirements for becoming a true virtuoso in the following manner:

1) The virtuoso must aspire to developing a consummate sense of deception. Remember, the hand is quicker than the eye, and the ear is the slowest of all. Learn to seem rather than to be. Remember your audience cares not a damn about what you can do, but it cares a lot about what you appear to do.

2) Develop a refined instinct for discerning the real wealth and true marital status of each member of your audience. Learn to spot rich, melancholy widows at sight.

3) Develop a dress characterized by shock effect. Hair styling here is of paramount importance. Never employ a barber or a comb. Dress down for all occasions, never up.

4) Cultivate boorishness into an art form remembering the example of the immoral Beethoven. The art of insult, the art of bizarre manners, and the art of gross public display are part of your expected image.

[20] The same as *The Trojans,* except that it is French.
[21] This may be a contradiction in terms.

5) Become a conductor. To learn an instrument requires some skill and to sing, some gift. To flail ones arms violently requires neither, and yet you remain center stage at all times.

6) Travel extensively. Remember you can deceive most of the people most of the time; some of the people all of the time; but there is always that one bastard who catches on. Be prepared to hit the road instantaneously when that happens.

7) Cultivate a religious tone. Religious ambience gives the other elements of your performance greater validity. Remember that Eastern mysticism is much superior to Western orthodoxy.

8) Remember that even humility can be a virtue if practiced judiciously. Learn to plead when in desperation, particularly when the sum involved exceeds one million francs.

In the figures of Nicololo Paganinini, the vileolinist, and Frans List, the fortissimo-pianist, we find the 19th century epitome of the virtuoso. Both mastered Mastdarm's text completely, and each had the added advantage of being able to play as well. Nicky wrote some of the most difficult and meaningless music ever written for the violin. One particular stunt dazzled his audiences more than any other. He would play a difficult composition through in the normal manner. He then would take out a pair of scissors, cut his E string, and play the composition again. Out would come the shears again, and there went the A string. Finally he would sever the D string and play the composition through on the G string alone. One evening, as he was doing this, his G string broke. He continued without interruption. The audience was enthralled. They clapped vigorously, as they had never heard such ethereal music before. As you can see, Paganinini has mastered Mastdarm's first precept completely. Nicky wrote a number of concertos for violin and orchestra.[22] All of them emphasize the violin. In fact the orchestra has little to play; and when it does do something, the dynamic markings are always pianissimo. Paganinini won the battle of the concerto by the simple expedient of silencing the orchestra. The glories of the military mind!

After having had an otherwise solid musical education, List encountered Paganinini. Nothing undoes a budding virtuoso more than the suggestion that he is being outdone. Frans immediately got to work writing music which he alone could play. Since it was necessary for him to

[22] There are no Paganinini concertos for bassoon and orchestra; one does not need to wonder why.

Paganinini, about to cut his G-string. What showmen these Italians are!!

play recitals every night and these had to be followed by seduction of one countess after another until the wee hours, Frans had little time for original composition. He, therefore, transcribed the works of every major composer for his novel pianistic idiom. Beethoven symphonies, Nicky's worthless trivia, arias by Mozart, an occasional ditty of Frans himself, and even the *Crucificux* from the *Mass in B Minor* of Bach became cannon fodder in the new musical war.

We are told that List's technique was prodigious. We have only the testimony of his many mistresses for this, but they were entitled to know. He must also have been able to play the piano pretty well, because Beethoven had kissed him on the cheek when he was young.[23] Some people said List played as if he had eleven fingers. Look at his pictures. You will observe his nose was long and sharp. Good virtuosi think of everything.

As he got older, List repented for his many sins in a long autobiographical work, *The Years of Pilgrimage.* In fact, his sins were so extensive that his publisher refused to place them in a single volume, and so there are two. Finally List turned to the priesthood in hopes he could avoid the stresses of mortal life. Was he in for a surprise!

When he became tired of doodling on the piano, List wrote a lot of symphonic music, although he never seemed able to put all the parts together to produce a true symphony.[24] In order to publish these pieces, he needed to call them something, and so he chose two terms which, although they are different, mean the same thing. The symphonic poem and the tone poem are similar, particularly considering that neither is a poem, they rarely have anything to do with poetry, and they both last much longer than any sonnet of which I know. In writing a symphonic poem,[25] the composer first writes an orchestral composition which meanders excessively. The themes are all poorly related to one another in the fashion of the stream of consciousness novel.[26] In music this is known as thematic metamorphosis, although thematic metamorbidity might do as well. Finally, when his composition is complete, the composer begins the truly important task of writing a program to fit the ill-contrived music. He hopes to see all manner of visual and poetic objects in the ambiguous musical texture. To accomplish this, the

[23] List was young, that is, not Beethoven.
[24] The minuet seemed to give him a lot of trouble.
[25] Or tone poem for that matter.
[26] Ask someone who knows something about literature to explain what is meant by the stream of consciousness novel. If he can do this, he knows more about Romanticism than is safe for the body politic.

List prepares to practice his technique and then the piano.

composer must wear a special pair of tri-focal, rose-colored glasses in order to achieve the correct effect. Reason must play no part, and afterwards the composer must insist that he began with the program in the first place. Music produced in this manner is particularly good for use in the background of Lone Ranger radio broadcasts.

Romantic Opera

As one might guess, it was in the field of opera that the romantics had their best day in court. For what they accomplished there, the judge should have imprisoned the entire lot of them for the entire nineteenth century. We have already observed that individuality was an important element of the romantic spirit. Individuality carried to the corporate political level explains nationalism, which is the concept that one's nation, under God, can do no wrong, even if it murders six million innocent persons. Nationalism led to different types of opera, all of them equally insane, but each with its own unique pathology.[27] Unfortunately, these various pathologies make this section of this book longer than it has any right to be.

German Magical Opera

The Germans had never had an opera of their own. Until the nineteenth century, they had been content to steal Italian opera, along with as much else belonging to the poor Italians as they could cart north of the Alps. With the advent of nationalism, such a condition could no longer be tolerated, so Carl Maria von Weber[28] invented German magical opera. Every opera in this species has its own magician, who may be a member of the cast, the composer sitting in the audience, the conductor, or even the serpent player. At the conclusion of the overture, which is always brilliant at the beginning but quiet at the end, the magician waves his magic wand, the audience is mesmerized into a dreamy sleep, and so remains until the last scene of the last act. For the last ten minutes of the opera, the composer writes a scene in which all the lovers are reconciled, the devil is chasted away, and the prize is awarded to the deserving young tenor.[29] The audience is always enthralled.

Weber's most successful opera was *Der Freistierschütz* (The Free Bullshooter), and its plot is

[27] Psychiatrists tell us that no two insane persons are insane in exactly the same fashion. The same is true of national operatic styles.

[28] Or Charlie Weaver, for short.

[29] One of the reasons German magical operas are rarely performed today is that deserving young tenors are about as rare as castrati.

typical of other operas in the genre. A magic bull has been terrorizing the village of Ochstadt, goring its maidens, and breaking into the Schlitz Malt Liquor Beer Hall. Max, the hero, decides to rid the town of this curse, but he doesn't know how. The Devil, disguised as a Prussian general, appears to Max and convinces him that the bull may only be slain by some magic bullets, which the general alone can cast. In return for this, Max agrees to allow Agatha, his beloved, to elope with the general, with whom she is madly in love. In the famous Ochsglen scene, Max meets the general at midnight in a frightening spot. The magic bullets are cast: "Ein! Zwei! Drei! Funf![30] Sex! Sieben! Acht! Neun! und ZEHN!" Then all hell breaks loose. Five hundred live bulls are unleashed on stage, the lights flicker and expire, the tympany player drums louder and louder, the violins play as many notes per minute as possible, the conductor turns cartwheels, and the theater manager goes bananas. The audience hopefully sleeps through it all, and they will if the bulls can be kept on stage. In the finale, Max fires the last of his ten magic bullets at the bull,[31] misses and hits the general. The bull, however, sights a cow he had been after all the time, and wanders harmlessly off the stage. Agatha is reconciled with Max in her famous aria, *Ich liebe dich,* in which she sings that there is nothing to be gained by being in love with a dead general. Everything ends happily for everyone. Weber, when he finished *Der Freistierschütz,* bemoaned the fact that he never would be able to do better. He never did.

French Grand Opera

In France the rage of the first half of the century was French grand opera, which differed from French comic opera only in the fact that it replaced spoken dialogue with sung recitative. As a result, the words could rarely be understood, but, since the words weren't too important anyway, it didn't make any difference. In grand opera, spectacles were what counted, the thicker the better. Each member of the audience was provided with specially machined glasses which magnified the stage by a factor of three. Everything, then, appeared larger than life. Everything was grandiose, and subtle nuance was banned by edict of the Faculté de le Conservatoire de Musique.[32] The director of the Paris Opera, Cecil B. De Mille, The First, sought throughout the world for unique stage effects which might stagger the already drunken French opera goers.

[30] German generals never can count! They can't spell either.
[31] He has previously missed nine times. He never did well in ROTC target practice.
[32] See the *Canons of the Conservatoire* for 1826, pp. 3089-3092, articles XXXXXXII and XXXXXXIII.

"Everything for effect," he said, and everyone who left the operas left feeling their effects very strongly.

The most important composer in the French grand opera tradition was the German, Giacomo Meyerbeer.[33] His father's name had merely been Beer, but his maternal grandfather, who was very rich, was named Meyer. For 300,000 francs, young Giacomo was persuaded to add Meyer to his name. From that time on, the composer was willing to alter anything, including an entire act of a opera, for the sum of 300,000 francs. Meyerbeer's most famous opera, *Roberta* or *The Hugenot Prophetess of Malta,* is a work of six hours in length, and is scored for an orchestra of one hundred and twenty players, two military bands, a drum and bugle corp, sixty-four majorettes, and a platoon of horsedrawn artillery.[34a] If it were possible, I would here recount the plot, but since one didn't exist in this work, I can only list in order the spectacles Giacomo envisaged in his opera:[33a]

1) the descent from the Alps by Hannibal and his elephants
2) the ascent of Mount Everest
3) the destruction of the Temple of Jerusalem
4) the crossing of the Red Sea
5) an eruption of Mount Etna
6) the Battle of Waterloo
7) man's landing on the moon
8) the Conquest of Peru
9) the storming of the Bastille
10) the ascension of Christ

About the musical style which underlay all these dramatic miracles, little need be said. The music could rarely be heard, even if one tried, and because there was so much to see, to listen would have been distracting. Meyerbeer was one of opera's most successful composers for the simple reason that he convinced his audiences largely to ignore the music he wrote.[34] He died wealthy, an accomplishment rarely attained by more exalted musical mentalities.

[33] Or Jack Beer, for short.

[34] The composer wanted to be assured that the work would be indeed grand.

[33a] The opera contains other spectacles too insignificant to mention.

[34a] Wagner described Meyerbeer's music as "a monstrous motley, historico-romantic, sacro-frivolous, mysterious brazen, sentimental-humbugging, dramatic potch." As they say, "it takes one, to spot one."

Italian Opera: The Singer Center Stage

The Italian view of opera was certainly as one sided as that of either the French or the Germans. The Italians had the silly idea that opera should be dominated by the singers and nobody else. The theory was that Italian audiences had come to the opera houses to hear the singers and for no other purpose. Simple observation would have proven that the audiences had come to munch on pasta, sip the latest vintages, throw pastrami at the conductor, hiss the basso, and chit-chat so fast no one could understand. Singers, however, have a universal ego problem which forces them center stage at all times, even when no one pays the slightest attention.

There was a peculiar requirement if one were to become proficient in writing Italian opera. That requirement was that one's name end with the letter "i". Rossini, Bellini, Donizetti, and Verdi were the principal composers for this type of opera, although less prominent figures in the field included Lombardi, Ernani, and Semiramidi. Rossini cranked out one Italian opera after another until he was the ripe old age of thirty-seven. He lived the next forty years in peace without darkening the door of an opera house. In the entire *Annals of Opera,* there is no other example of a composer who underwent a similar "Pauline" experience.

Donizetti, who was noted for his acute perception (especially when he stepped on a tack), noted that the writing of Italian opera was easy; it was the rehearsals which were difficult. He said nothing about having to sit through one. Bellini wrote pretty melodies which sounded just like Chaikovsky.[35] Bellini's one attempt to write in the grand opera tradition, *Enorma* (1834), failed miserably, and the young composer died the next year in disgrace.

Verdi, however, was certainly the master of nineteenth century Italian opera. He stands head and shoulders above his rivals. In fact he stands from the ankles upwards above them. His masterpiece is, of course, *Aïda,* which was written for the dedication of the Suez Canal. The task of digging the canal was infinitely easier than that of writing a good Italian opera. As a result Verdi was late, and the canal had to open without him or his opera. The famous Nile scene opens with crickets, and, if it is done outdoors in the summer time, as it often is, with mosquitoes, too. In this scene Aïda, who is an Ethiopian captive and handmaiden for her hated mistress, Amneris, who is Egyptian and the queen, pleads with her lover, Radames, who is also Egyptian and a prince, to flee with her to Ethiopia. Just why Radames, who had it made in Egypt and would be a

[35] Perhaps this is the reason Chaikovsky sounds so much like Bellini.

nobody in Ethiopia, would have even entertained such a thought is not too clear, but Aïda persuades him in any case. As they flee, they meet Amonastro, Aïda's father, who is not about to allow his daughter to go home with any Egyptian. Radames and Amonastro fight a duel, and the older man trips, falls into the Nile, and is devoured by the crocodiles.[36] Aïda is now enraged, and has Radames, whom she now hates,[37] imprisoned for murder. In the last act all is reconciled. Radames and Aïda are sealed in a tomb, where they can carry on to their hearts' content without anyone knowing what they are up to, except the audience. Italian love affairs always have weird endings. As one can readily see, the libretti of Italian operas are filled with situations of deep human passion, considerable violence, and grim sexual overtones. The moral majority would have had a field day with any one of them.

In the last years of his life, Verdi turned to Shakespeare for his inspiration. Foreigners have a difficult time pronouncing the English sound represented by the letters "th." So Verdi's *Othello* came out as *Otello,* and it has been that way ever since. Save for this small deficiency, it is a very successful work. His final opera, *Falstaff,* is based on Shakespeare's play, the *Merry Wives of Verona.* Verdi ended this opera with a serious fugue on the text: "Tutto nel mondo e burla" (All the world's a joke). To live through seventy-seven years of writing Italian operas would require some sense of humor. It is lucky Verdi died in 1901. To have lived further into the twentieth century would have been to discredit his point of view.

Richard Wagner und das Gesamtkunstwerk

It is necessary that we devote an entire section to a discussion of the works of Richard Wagner for the simple reason that he stands as the most important personality of the entire nineteenth century. We know this for certain, because he told us so himself. Wagner was largely self taught. No one could teach him a thing when he was young, and the habit stuck with him until the day he died. He began his career by writing operas in each of the major traditions we have just discussed: *Das Feen* (The Fiend), in the style of von Weber; *Leibesverbot* (The Forbidden Body), in the style of Donizetti; and *Rienzi, the Flying Dutchman,* in the style of Meyerbeer. Each opera failed miserably at its first performance, and Wagner was routinely chased out of town by a lynch mob after each attempt. He was finally exiled to Switzerland, where there was no opera

[36] Or was it alligators? I can't remember.
[37] Women can be fickle, particularly when you murder their fathers.

tradition for him to ruin. Here he was befriended by List, who loaned the composer a mistress or two with whom he could pass his idyll hours.

Wagner, who underwent a spiritual regeneration during his Swiss exile,[38] decided that if he couldn't write successful opera, the task was not worth the trouble. What counted was MUSIC DRAMA, and he would try his hand at that. Wagner said there had already been too much opera composition, and with that, no one would have disagreed. What he did not make too clear, however, was that each of his MUSIC DRAMAS was to be the equivalent of six operas in any other tradition.

In his MUSIC DRAMAS, Wagner was concerned with developing the *Gesamtkunstwerk* (The Consumptive Art Work), in which all the arts would be blended into a super art, all under the direction of Herr Wagner. His goal was to do in MUSIC DRAMA what Hitler attempted eighty years later with the Third Reich. Everyone had to be subservient to Richard, and, if you dared not to be, you would find yourself permanently cast as a fool in his next major production.

Wagner realized that of all the personnel required in MUSIC DRAMA, the singers would be the most difficult to control. He reasoned that if the major action happened off stage in the orchestra pit, his control would be easier to effect. You must look toward the orchestra for the action, where, during the performance of a Wagner work, one can see the string bass players using their instruments as bows and shooting arrows at the singers, the cymbal player catching his nose between his discs, horn players forming pyramids while blowing one bugle call after another, violin players climbing over one another's backs to become concertmaster, and the tuba player catching his thumb in the crooks of his tubing. Only the harp players seem uninvolved. They always act angelic.

The musical structure of a Wagner opera is held together by *Leidmotivs.*[39] Every major character had his own *Leidmotiv*. Good, evil, heroism, the holy grail, magic swords, and other such nonsense, each receives its own *motiv*. You can understand what is happening in the drama if you know the *motivs*. If you do not, you will become certainly lost, but, then, the conductor is almost certainly lost himself, so it makes very little difference.

Wagner's melodic structure is called continuous melody. This means that when a melody

[38] The romantics routinely went through spiritual regenerations which rarely were of much use.

[39] An exact translation of this term is impossible in English. The literal translation, "motives of sorrow" does not carry exactly the correct connotation.

starts, as they have a habit of doing early in the overtures, it will continue uninterrupted until the conclusion of that act. As more and more melodies are introduced, more and more melodic strands become simultaneously active, and the sound grows thicker and thicker. Since each act lasts at least six hours, it is necessary to protect one's ears during the last two by the use of ear muffs. These are normally sold in the theater lobby along with the four hundred page libretti, which are characteristic of Wagner MUSIC DRAMAS.

Wagner's masterpiece is *The Ring,* a cycle of operas with a deceptively simple name for a work of such arcane meaning. In writing *The Ring,* Wagner began backwards. He began with the last scene of the fourth opera and gradually worked back to the prelude of the first opera. It took him over twenty-five years to complete the work.[40] While the details of the story are far too complex for us to relate here in our limited space, we can say that the cycle revolves around a magic ring, which can cure all the ills of the world.[41] The ring was given to Siegfried by Wotan at the beginning of the cycle. The ring is lost during the dimness caused by the Twilight of the Gods *(Götterdammerung),* and for the next two dramas, the action revolves around its recovery. In the last drama, the ring is discovered wedged into the shoe of one the horses belonging to the Valkyries. In a great festive ceremony the ring is awarded to Brunnhilde, who vows to wear it proudly until the next performance of *The Ring,* when it can become lost again.

The Ring was such a monumental work that Wagner despaired of ever having it performed. He was turned down by every opera house in the Western hemisphere. Each director said his house performed operas, not MUSIC DRAMAS. Since the composer had no money, and opera houses, particularly those on a Wagnerian scale, are rather expensive, Richard was in tears. At just the right moment, the young king Ludwig II came to the throne of Bavaria. He gave Wagner a blank check, which the composer filled in for an amount which nearly bankrupted the country.[42] In the little Bavarian village of Buyright, Wagner had his famous theater constructed. Everyone flocked there in the summers to hear *The Ring* and to buy souvenir programs, which listed all the *Leidmotivs.* Some people do the weirdest things on their vacations.

Wagner's most appealing opera is his immortal *Tristan und Isolde.* The opera has one unique advantage. One can successfully perform the prelude and skip directly to the final scene, the

[40] It takes just a little less time to perform it.
[41] It is doubtful that it could have cured Wagnerism.
[42] We can forgive Ludwig for this indiscretion. He was only eighteen and insanity ran in his family.

Wagner composing the text for one of his Music Dramas. The first scene of the first act is stacked a few feet in front of him.

famous love death, which can be done as well without the singers. In so doing, the audience is spared the singers, six hours of *Leidmotivs,* most of the garbage of the *Gesamtkunstwerk* theory, and most of the action in the orchestra pit. The work is generally performed in this manner.

Before we leave Wagner, something your author has been wanting to do since he was ten years of age, we should make what positive comments we can about his infamous personality:

Nationalism and the Romantic Movement

We have already encountered nationalism in our discussion of opera. If that had been the only place it cropped up, it might have been ignored, but it had its effects on all idioms of nineteenth century music.[43] In order to be a nationalistic composer, it was necessary to be born in a country struggling to establish and maintain its identity, and in the nineteenth century, that included all nations except France, England, or Prussia. Composers were forced to spend as much time as possible in the wild collecting folksongs, which they incorporated into their music at every inappropriate moment. Nationalistic composers were expected to employ local color in their works. Not only did they write with gaudy inks, but performances of their works were characterized by all manner of outlandish, but colorful costumes.[44] Composers were expected to make use of native dancers, and dancing girls, too, if they were available. All performances were required to begin with the national anthem, a fireworks display, and the pledge of allegiance to the flag.

[43] Particularly music for military band.

[44] The violins of the National Bohemian Orchestra were all painted in pastel shades.

Chopin recuperating on Majorca. The "lady" in the picture is actually George Sand, dressed as Madame Dudevant. Chopin himself is incognito, disguised as Hoagy Carmichael.

Nationalistic music was common in the Balkan countries,[45] in Scandinavia,[46] and even in the United States, where much excellent music was written during the century.[47] One of the most important of all composers, who showed strong traits of nationalism, was the Polish composer Frederic Chopin, whose name is always mispronounced by musical illiterates. He loved his native land so intensely that he left it at age nineteen and never returned. His music is all for the piano, which shows what genius can sometimes accomplish if it does not go off in all directions. The Polish national influence is shown in Chopin's many dances, particularly the polonaise[48] and the majurka. His creative life was spent in Paris, save for one year he spent on the Isle of Majorca recuperating from an illness caused by his love affair with George Sand, an English novelist, who, under the name of Mme. Dudevant, posed as a woman. That Chopin's genius was not appreciated in this day is certainly evident from a comment of another Englishman who gave Chopin trouble. John Field, who should have read a popular poem of Robert Burns and left Chopin alone, said, "his genius is of a sick, chamber order." The last days of our sensitive composer were spent in poverty. His only employment was to be found playing bar room piano in the saloons of Paris. Here, his scherzi, which weren't very funny, could hardly have been appreciated. Some amends were made after his death. He was buried between Cherubini and Bellini. Both should have been honored.

Nowhere was nationalism more important than in Russia. Since the days of Peter the Gross, Russia had been trying to keep her national identity while consorting with the whore of European culture.[49] The tension this produced was felt strongly in the training, or lack thereof, of every Russian composer. In the latter half of the century a group of "composers," Balakirev, Borodin, Cui, Mussorgsky, the Rimsky-Korsakov,[50] organized themselves into a group known by the imaginative name of *The Five.* None was a professional musician but that was regarded as a virtue, not a vice. *The Five* were particularly adamant that no true Russian music could be produced by anyone who knew anything about music, particularly by anyone who knew anything

[45] Where there was always an identity crisis.
[46] Where all the colors used were warm.
[47] Since it was written on the wrong side of the Atlantic, it didn't count.
[48] Chopin, who was also a gourmet cook, invented a sauce of the same name.
[49] It was a little like avoiding herpes in an American College.
[50] Any student who can name them gets an A minus. If they are spelled correctly, he gets an A plus.

about harmony and counterpoint.[51] These subjects were German, and they should be avoided in the same way as Bismarck's army. Ignorance was regarded as bliss, so blissful that one could sleep through an entire *Night on Bald Mountain* or an entire month *On the Steppes of Central Asia* without being interrupted by a single moment of professional competence.

The one Russian composer of the century, who refused to apply for admission to the company of *The Five*[52] was Piotr Ilyitch Chaikovsky, who had his name listed under "T" in the Moscow telephone directory so he wouldn't get so many annoying calls. Chaikovsky, who made A's in harmony and counterpoint, wasn't going to deny his accomplishments for one minute, even if everyone called him a German and addressed him as "Meinherr." He said he would use folk songs if and when he wanted to, and he would use black ink if it suited him. But, as we all know, he was a peculiar man who didn't want to go along with the crowd.

He was determined to write symphonies, and he wrote three, which nobody paid the slightest attention to. He decided no one would ignore his fourth. He would make it so loud everyone would have to listen, and he would include a march to which everyone could relate.[53] The symphony succeeded, and it established Chaikovsky as the greatest of the Russian symphonists.[54]

Chaikovsky was lucky to have had a benefactress throughout his life, a Madame von Muck, whom he milked for all she was worth, which was plenty. They never met, although The Madame suggested it several times. Each time Chaikovski would reply, by letter, that he didn't relate well to women, and such a meeting might prove injurious to the relationship. In this Chaikovsky was right. He had already driven his wife into an insane asylum. Madame Muck, who just didn't know how to be hurt, continued to pay the bills until the composer was famous and rich. Some people have all the luck.

During this last years, Chaikovsky became more and more depressed. He then launched into writing his last and most pathetic symphony. By this time he was so deranged, that he deranged the order of the movements and ended his symphony with the slow, depressing finale, which dragged the entire symphony and its composer into the mire of a cholera epidemic then raging

[51] The same point of view is maintained by present-day rock musicians.
[52] He wouldn't have been admitted anyway. *The Five* didn't want to change its name.
[53] Everyone, except rock musicians, can relate to marches. They can't relate to anything.
[54] Shostokovitch envied this reputation and tried to put an end to it fifteen times.

in Moscow. As he finished the last notes, the composer drank a glass of unboiled water, and died a pathetic death, with pen in hand. His mother had also died of drinking unboiled water in the middle of a cholera epidemic. There was a peculiarly defective gene in the family strain somewhere.

Reason in the Midst of Dementia: Classicism in the Romantic Period

Throughout the nineteenth century, there existed a musical underground of classicism. The old-fashioned composers who contributed to this development met together in underground cellars in Leipzig and Vienna, in attempts to avoid Wagner's *Musikalischestaatspolizei* (Mustapo), an early precursor of Hitler's *Gestapo*. When Wagner was out of town, due to an exile, they would emerge from the sewers, organize concerts of the music they had just written underground, attract what persons of reason were still alive, and thoroughly enjoy music. Meanwhile, they kept close scrutiny on Richard's movements.

The most important composers in this tradition were Felix Mendelssohn,[55] Robert Schumann,[56] but, most of all, Johannes Brahmins. Brahmins said that he could see, early in his life, where *Leidmotivs* could lead one, and he didn't want to go there. Instead, he intended to write the tenth symphony. He spent the next fifteen years writing his first. At that rate the task would have taken a century and a half, so Brahmins gave up after his fourth attempt.

Brahmins was a lovely old man,[57] who took walks in the Vienna woods,[58] sang lullabies to all his grandchildren,[59] and looked like Santa Claus. As he walked, he kept looking over his shoulder at the past, where the ghost of Beethoven haunted him until his death. He once attempted to write an opera, *The Academic Festival*, but never finished more than the overture. He hated to travel, and once turned down a doctorate at Oxford, because he didn't want to go to England. Most persons wouldn't turn down a doctorate at Oxford if they had to travel by rocket to Pluto. Brahmins was Brahmins!

[55] Whose first name means "happy." You'd be happy, too, if your father were rich and had given you your very own orchestra to play with at age fourteen.

[56] Whose attempts to be classic and romantic at the same time led to an insane asylum.

[57] He was old at fourteen.

[58] Where he met Johann Strauss.

[59] Although he was never married.

Chaikovsky unwittingly (?) gargles cholera tainted water.

His music had a touch of the past in it. One can find Bach, Haydn, Beethoven, hemiolas, passacaglias, and Phrygian modes hanging their heads out of it. Musicologists like to point these things out. Otherwise, his music produced pleasure for just about everybody except Wagner, and that is just what it was intended to do for everybody except Wagner. Wagner called Brahmins "the chaste Johannes." Just how Richard knew anything about Johannes' limited sex life, I do not know. But, then, Wagner knew something nasty about every nice person in the nineteenth century!

Somnolence, Impressionism, and Debussy

For the last paroxysm of the romantic movement we must return to France, where, in music, Berlioz had started it all. During the last years of the nineteenth century, the entire French intellectual community, from painters and musicians to Clemenceau himself, wore its rose-colored glasses twenty-four hours a day. Everyone sought to obtain the vaguest impression of what was going on around him, and no one had the slightest wish to understand the realities of the world. Perhaps such an escape from reality was explicable in view of a world twiddling its thumbs awaiting the Kaiser, his armies, and the horrors of the imminent war. This desire to impress upon oneself only an impression of reality finds its counterpart in the arts in Impressionism, a doctrine of the arts which sought to blur everything. The music of Claude Debussy, the arch musical impressionist (although he could not be impressed into admitting it), not only blurs everything, it confuses everything as completely as possible.

Debussy is another of the world's great composers who had no roots. He hated everything: his parents, the church, Bach and Beethoven, symphonies, Germans, work, and harmony classes. One day, as he was playing his harmony exercise through for Durand, his theory professor at LeCon Servatoire, Durand slammed the piano lid right down on Debussy's hands. Not only did Debussy's career as a budding piano virtuoso come to an end, but his interest in conventional harmony and Durand's class came to an end, as well. Debussy defied his teacher. He made it clear he would write as many parallel fifths as he wanted, he would use dissonant chords any way they suited him, he wouldn't raise the seventh degree of a minor scale if he didn't want to, and he wouldn't resolve dominant seventh chords in a proper fashion. Some theory students overreact to the slightest criticism.

To understand Debussy and his music we must understand something of his personality. In the first place, he was lazy. In the few hours each day during which he was awake, he liked to sit

Brahmins' dislike of Wagner is evident in the decor of his bathroom.

around and take in as many sensuous moments as possible.[60] The most famous picture of him shows a rather rotund, dark-bearded figure, lolling in a Bentwood rocker, being served beverages by a serving girl in oriental dress.[61] Whenever he got out of his Bentwood, he would meander to the nearest cafe, where he would sit, sip coffee or something stronger, and chat with anyone who came along, as long as the conversations contained only impressions and no facts.

We must describe Debussy's unique method of composition. First he conjured up a possible subject for meditation. This might be the sea, the Spanish countryside, a girl with flax for hair, or the wanderings of a deer on a summer afternoon. He would, then, have his Bentwood carried to a proper spot, where he could observe his selected phenomenon until the spirit moved him to convert his observations into musical impressions. As he worked on his famous *L'après-midi d'un faune,* he had his chair mounted on the back of a truck, which he had driven around following a single deer for an entire afternoon. The driver thought Claude to be some peculiar hunter who had forgotten his rifle. The length the composer would go to achieve his ends leaves one an impression of a very devoted impressionist. In writing his *Engulfed Cathedral,* Debussy had his Bentwood installed in a diving bell, and he and his rocker were lowered into the Mediterranean off the island of Malta, where he could be impressed by an ancient, submerged church on the sea floor.

In order to convert his sensuous visions into musical parallels, it was necessary for Debussy to destroy conventional music, which he didn't like, couldn't understand, and wouldn't fit his purposes in the least. How could one make a sonata or a fugue conform to the images of a fool deer? To this end, Debussy invented a new musical language, which he alone understood and spoke with fluency. All manner of unusual sounds, strange harmonies, borrowings from the medievil past, odd scales, and weird instruments were used to effect just the proper nuance in the composer's search for musical impressions.[62]

To listen to such a unique musical language requires equally unique procedures. One begins by consuming a half pint of any rich liqueur;[63] one then rocks sensuously for another half hour

[60] None of Debussy's several love affairs ever came to much. As soon as he lay down on a bed, he fell immediately to sleep.

[61] Debussy liked oriental dress. He regarded it as sensuous.

[62] He replaced conventional musical forms by blocks of sound, which he put together in exactly the way a four-year-old puts blocks together, haphazardly.

[63] Although it is rarely available, absinthe is preferred.

in a Bentwood rocker; then one turns on the phonograph very softly at the beginning of *L'après-midi.* Gradually the volume should be increased until it is just a little below normal. One should, then, begin to dream. If a dream about a silly deer doesn't come to mind, that about a gerbil will do as well. As one falls into a deep slumber, one's roommate covers one up in a warm blanket, turns out the lights and the record player, and then lights an incense candle. One wakes up the next morning refreshed. Debussy said that Berlioz was the favorite composer of those who knew nothing about music. He had not lived long enough to appreciate the effects of his own musical style on the musically ignorant. Debussy did live long enough to observe the effects of German cannons aimed at Paris in 1918. The impression these made on him could not be converted into music, and the composer, therefore, promptly died.

Debussy was one of the earliest fatalities which resulted from mixing nineteenth century Romanticism with twentieth century Barbarism. A new age had begun; it hasn't ended yet; and there are no signs it may do so any time soon.

Chapter VII

Music in the Twentieth Century or Why Anyone is Justified in Saying He Hates Modern Music

Debussy had slept into the twentieth century, but the German cannons had awakened even him for the last few hours of his life. The blood-red events of the First World War were made even redder when viewed through rose-colored glasses, and wearing them went rapidly out of style. As one person after another took off his glasses, only to have them immediately pulverized by the tread of a German tank, he discovered a world he wished he had never seen. Despite the advances in modern optical technology, our century had invented no glasses which much improve our view of it, and, since research in glasses is out and research in computers is in, it is unlikely that any are to be invented.

Our century has been involved in one technological innovation after another. Our success here has been so stunning that it is a commonplace observation that man's moral sense cannot keep up with technological advance. For that matter, man's moral sense has not kept up with technology since the invention of the wheel. We are now able to go almost anywhere in the solar system at undreamed of speeds without any motive for going there in the first place. After all, a society, which can remove the water from orange juice and satisfactorily replace it before the consumer is aware of its absence cannot be all bad. Our capacity for mass self-destruction is truly admirable, and some day we may find a productive purpose for it. We have already directed this technology toward peace by fighting the bloodiest wars in the history of our planet. We are assured we have the capability to kill everyone on earth twenty times over, although no one is certain who will remain for the second round of fire, much less the twentieth. But there is no need to worry; man's reason has shown forth in the past, and will, no doubt, do so with equal fervor in the future.

Modern music has kept up with these great strides in technology. Many times it has joined forces with the technocrats under the theory that what's good for General Motors is also what's good for music. While the Impressionists slept, other musicians decided to put an end to all music which people could enjoy. Music which contained a single singable melody was degenerate, and any which contained a single consonant chord had to be the work of such conservative minds as would advocate the divine right of kings. There was an effort to remove from music every vestige of a positive attitude towards the world, to dehumanise musical structures, to emphasize the noisy environment of the modern world, and to force music to keep up-to-date with the contemporary world. If, as a composer, you choose not to go along with such foolishness, you were branded as hopelessly reactionary and accused of wearing your rose-colored glasses as you composed. It is no wonder that normal persons,[1] who seek to find solace in music, should have decided to let modern music go to hell, where it probably was headed anyway. Instead they have chosen to listen to an outdated repertory which had little to do with a world which had readily killed fifty million of its inhabitants in the search for peace.[2]

Atoneality

It is actually not too difficult to remove harmony and melody from music. Let any three year old loose on a piano keyboard and it will not take him two minutes to figure that out. What is difficult, however, is to preserve music after harmony and melody have been taken away. That is exactly the problem encountered by serious[3] composers in the first quarter of the twentieth century. One of the most interesting solutions, and unfortunately one of the more enduring, was hit upon by the English composer, Arnold Beaumont (1874-1951), whose works were fortunately never printed. As he ate his alphabet soup one evening, he realized that all those arbitrary letters were just the ones he was using in music. How could he successfully keep them all scrabbled up, and yet make sense of them, all at the same time?[4] Beaumont spent a restless night turning the problem over and over in his head and himself over and over in his bed. No solution seemed evident, until suddenly, while eating his cream-of-wheat the next morning at breakfast, the answer came to him.[5] All the twelve notes would be tossed into a hat. Then, one after another,

[1] That is persons who are not contemporary composers.

[2] The split of audiences from the contemporary repertory is often bemoaned. It is actually one of the few signs of sanity in the present-day musical world.

[3] That is those who were not laughing under their hats.

[4] As you can see, twentieth century composers are faced with inordinate intellectual difficulties.

[5] The solution has always been termed the "cereal technique" after the unusual circumstances surrounding its discovery.

they would be drawn out and lined up in a row. The resulting tone row would then be used over and over until a composition came to an end, or all the audience had left, whichever came first.

It was rapidly discovered that if one threw the tone row up in the air and caught it upside down, one would have two related rows, and if one looked at each of these in the mirror, four cousins would exist. If you multiplied four by twelve, you got forty-eight. Each row had twelve notes, and twelve times forty-eight gave five hundred and seventy-six notes, which was more than enough to write in any incomprehensible style.[6] The sins of Beaumont's creation were so great, that the style became known as atoneality, or the music for which its composers will be perpetually atoning.

The cereal technique adapted itself readily to expressing the dark and pathological emotions of the twentieth century, and particularly the dark and pathological emotions of soap operas and horror movies. It was immediately adopted by a host of fifth-rate composers, who know and care much more for cereal than they do for music. Such composers love to put notes in a hat, shake them up, toss them in the air, and allow them to land anywhere on the music paper that chance decrees. Such composers, we hope, will spend the rest of time atoning for their sins in purgatory. Heaven itself can hardly afford the risk of allowing them to run loose.

Barbarism and Primitivism

Considering the nature of our world, that barbarism has become a part of our music seems only two natural. Since westerners consider themselves sophisticated[7] and hardly barbaric, we have tended to attribute this barbarism to our contacts with the non-western world. Any westerner will tell you the non-western world is primitive,[8] so, then, it was natural for western composers to search there for a base for their barbarity. There was a procedure for composers to study non-western culture. A European composer applied for a grant-in-aid and traveled to some exotic place such as the Congo or New Guinea. There he dressed up in outlandish costumes, and took part in the local tribe's rites of spring. If the composer were American, he didn't need to bother with all of this. He could merely travel to exotic Fort Lauderdale over spring

[6] Cereal composers are always taken with their mathematical skills.
[7] The western world's capacity for self destruction is certainly sophisticated.
[8] It never developed a sophisticated capacity for self-destruction.

vacation.[9] After the composer had absorbed all the primitivism necessary to explain his inherent native barbarism, he returned home lugging along a half dozen native death masks to prove he had been away, to use on Halloween, and to decorate his Art Deco living room the remainder of the year.[10]

Immediately upon returning home, the composer scheduled a lecture, complete with slides, most of which contained pictures of the composer in native dress, and tapes, most of which were full of native insect and bird calls. Midway through his lecture, the composer announced what everyone had been waiting for: he was no longer going to be tyrannized by the bar line.[11] What that meant was that the composer had gotten tired of counting 1, 2, 3 - 1, 2, 3 - 1, 2, 3 and now wanted to count 1, 2 - 1, 2, 3 - 1, 2, 3, 4 - 1, 2 - 1, 2, 3 - 1, 2, 3, 4.[12] If he could mix all these up, he would be even more sophisticated or primitive, depending how you looked at it. To compose, now meant merely to take any notes, the more cacophonous the better, and to repeat them over and over in one of these assymmetrical rhythms, beginning as softly as possible and gradually making a crescendo until the fortissississississimo at the conclusion of the piece. By this time the sensitivities of the audience, assuming they existed in the first place, would be dulled, the hall would be rocking, all conservatives would have had the good sense to leave, and, if the performance had really been a success, some good-looking socialite would be taking off her cloths in the aisle. Most modern audiences can acquire a taste for barbaric primitivism if just given a chance, but there is always that stodgy symphony board which stands in the way of modern repertory.

At the conclusion of the performance, there was yet one more primitive ritual to be enacted. The one radical member of the symphony board, after she had retrieved her clothing from the primitive males who had been egging her on a few minutes earlier, threw a party in her stylish apartment.[13] The more primitive members of the audience were always invited, and the only distinct sound which could be heard above the primitive cacaphony were the "darrrlings" coming from the hostess' greetings. A punch made from a primitive recipe brought back from the Congo was served along with hors d'oeuvres, such as roast loin of boa constrictor. The composer arrived

[9] Or he could contact the head of the local rock band.

[10] Native tribes maintain healthy cottage industries producing such masks, which have nothing to do with their culture, but satisfy westerners.

[11] It was really his wife who was tyrannizing him ever since she found out about that native dancing girl.

[12] No composer can count past four.

[13] It is also decorated with primitive masks bought at Bloomingdales.

in his native dress. The conductor arrived in his equally barbaric native dress, white tie and tails. Everyone raved, and urged the hostess to repeat her highly successful performance. This she did to set the stage for others to follow.[14] At 4:00 A.M. the police raid the place; the reporter from the New York Times arrives; and the entire evening is proclaimed a huge success.

Expressionism

Closely related to atonealism, barbarism, and primitivism was the new artistic creed of expressionism. Until the twentieth century, men of culture and breeding, and a few women, too, had tried to keep their emotions in check. It was not too difficult to understand that only disaster could ensue in a society which allowed everyone to go around emoting as he or she damn well pleased. Most parents had tried to instill in junior some sense of emotional proprieties, and wild, spontaneous outbursts were normally forbidden in the young, even in public restaurants, well into the present century. The latter part of the nineteenth century brought us, along with a number of other catastrophic intellectual movements, the advent of psychiatry and the work of Sigmund Freud. He pointed out that emotions were an all right thing, and to cry in public wasn't the end of the world. Other public emotional explosions were all right, too, if one worked them out beforehand on Sigmund's couch.

Expressionism in art is merely the belief that to let everything in one's emotional life be bared in public is the only possible artistic truth. Bach, Palacetrina, Haydn, and Couperin would have been out of a job in five minutes if any of them had even thought such a thing. But times had changed. It would seem that the expressionists had been repressing a lot of negative feelings, because when they were at last allowed to let go what emerged was fear, anger, horror, fright, terror, hostility, apathy, and indifference. It is difficult to find a single expressionist who ever expressed love, delight, happiness, laughter, or joy. The expressionists normally employed the atoneal technique in its most chaotic and dissonant forms. Their training ground was either an insane asylum or viewing the *Exorcist* forty times without a break. Their compositional technique was simple. They exposed themselves to such horror until just the moment of the breaking point. They then hastened to take pen and paper, and, instead of screaming, they transferred the emotional outburst to paper.

One technical device associated with expressionistic style is called *Brechstimme,* or singing in a

[14] Primitivism is easy to imitate. It can be fun, too, if you can avoid herpes.

broken voice. To train himself to write good *Brechstimme,* the composer spent a month working on the docks at Camden, New Jersey or driving an eighteen wheeler from Saint Louis to Omaha. If neither were possible, he could spend a short week living in any American college dormitory. During this training period, he acquired a vocabulary laced with every obscene expression known to man or woman. *Brechstimme* consists of interpolating such obscenities into the musical structure in a voice which neither sings nor speaks. The device is reserved for expressing the most horrendous of emotional traumas.

One peculiarity of expressionist composers is the dismay they always feel when audiences walk out of their performances. Why, such composers ask, does no one understand? Why doesn't anyone want to listen? The answer is, of course, too simple[15] for the composers' minds. No one wants to listen to emotional outbursts, and it matters not a bit if they come from two year olds or thirty year olds. These composers should realize that good psychiatrists get two hundred dollars an hour for listening to persons bare their emotional lives. Why should the musical public be asked to pay for the experience.

Neoism

It was fortunate that barbarism, primitivism, atonealism, and expressionism did not suit the tastes of every composer of the early half of the twentieth century. There was still some reason left; a few musicians understood what a melody sounded like; a few enjoyed beautiful sounds; and there were even some who cared about such outdated matters as harmony, counterpoint, and formal order. Some composers still listened to Bach, Mozart, Chopin, and Brahmins and were brave enough to admit that such music could still be an inspiration. In order to receive a union card in composition, it has been necessary for every twentieth century composer to list the cult to which he belongs. Since such conservative composers had no cult of their own, they banded together into a group known as the neoists. When Bach and Handel were their inspiration they became neo-Broquists. When Haydn and Mozart were their inspiration they were known as neo-Classicists. When Brahmins and Chaikovsky were the inspiration they were neo-Romantics.[16] These composers went around hauling out of musical closets what little sanity remained stored there, airing it out, patching it up, remaking the garments, and wearing them

[15] Expressionist composers always try to be complicated and complex.
[16] That is reactionaries.

again. Occasionally, it was fun to write a symphony in classical style and pawn it off as one written by Mozart. Since Mozart wasn't around to protest and the musicologists hadn't studied the manuscripts,[17] these frauds were often left unchallenged.

Of course, no really good composer merely copies the past, and these neoists didn't either. Their music goes along sounding very similar to Mozart or Haydn. Then the composer throws in just enough weird harmony to make the work sound modern. He then returns to the safety of the past. This keeps happening through one piece after another. To the listener, the result is something like a movie going in and out of focus. The music sounds just mildly pathological, just enough to qualify as modern.[18]

The laudible, but nonetheless futile, efforts of the Neoists to preserve a degree of sanity in the musical world came to an end with the advent of World War II, when all sanity in every worldly endeavor likewise came to an end. There were those who felt that what had happened to music before 1940 was a disaster. Words cannot describe what those same persons thought when they witnessed music after the war, much less the physical state of Europe. What we have had is disaster followed by catastrophe.

Post World War II: The Avant Guard and The Caging of Music

The avant guard is a segment of an army which marches on ahead; even if it has lost its compasses and maps; hasn't the slightest idea where it is going much less where it has been; doesn't know at whom it is shooting; and leads everyone behind along the same paths. The results of the avant guard, in war or anywhere else, is always a geometric progression of Murphy's law. The avant guard had successfully marched through Europe and systematically destroyed a good part of it. After the war it could hardly stop marching and destroying, and music turned out to be an excellent arena for its new endeavors.

The following attributes are characteristic of composers in this new movement:[19]

1) They have always flunked out of a major music school because they hated their theory teacher, who loved Bach.

[17] Musicologists never listen to music when they make judgments. They study manuscripts.

[18] It is very necessary that all composers in our century sound modern. To sound modern is a requirement for receiving a university appointment with tenure. It is not necessary to learn harmony or counterpoint.

[19] The neodestructionists.

2) They invariably hate the environment in which they grew up. If it were an urban one, they hate the crassness of city life. If it were rural, they bemoan their lack of contact with the mainstreams of intellectual life.[20]

3) They always play some musical instrument badly. Generally it is the piano, which they modify to sound worse than it originally did.

4) They always hate the musical instrument which they can't play, because it inhibits their musical creativity.

5) They hate McDonald's hamburgers and love alfalfa seeds.

6) They hate popular American culture but love the affluence it provides particularly in the persons of rich widows, who fawn over them and line their pocketbooks with those horrid American dollars.

7) They love to speak French poorly.

8) They always have apartments in abandoned firehouses, with whitewashed walls, and a single piece of furniture, a non-descript affair, which serves as a bed, couch, and dining table, all at the same time.

9) Their musical scores look exactly like the abstract art work hanging on the walls of the firehouses. In fact, the two are interchangeable.

10) Their concerts are experiences, usually traumatic experiences, haunted by the ghost of Franz Kaufka.

11) They regard owning a razor or a comb to be forsaking their destinies. To own a necktie is a heresy which merits suicide.

12) They are in love with modern dance and particularly with the nubile young things who do bumps and grinds in the name of high art.

13) They avidly hate one another. This is the one attribute of the avant guard which is positive. Otherwise they would engage in a conspiracy which would make the red menace seem trivial in comparison.

[20] The fact that they cut themselves off from all streams of any intellectual life is a fact that they let go unnoticed.

The avant guard has always insisted on the necessity of audiences developing new modes of hearing. They demand an increase in auditory consciousness. They demand the acceptance of a much wider format of sound sources. To these ends, the concert situation has been recreated, and it may provide, for the more conventional concert goer, something of a shock.[21]

Some composers have chosen to ignore conventional musical instruments, and in doing so, have really done little harm. Those who have chosen to destroy those instruments have done more than their share. In the mid-1950's it was fashionable to have collections of instruments of all kinds heaped onto the stage and systematically transformed into debris by the composer/performer playing the sledge hammer. The subtle difference in timbre between a piano sound board being splintered and a tuba bell being smashed was an expansion of auditory consciousness which could hardly be ignored.

Other composers have chosen to use conventional instruments, but to use them in unconventional ways. For instance, the German composer, Rudolf von Kleinverstand, has a composition for wind ensemble which requires all the players to blow into their instruments through the bells throughout the entire composition. The result is a musical analog to looking into a telescope through the wrong end. The dynamic markings in the players scores come out in reverse as the music emerges from the mouthpieces of the instruments. In another example of this important composer's work, he requires the string instrument players to blow across the strings to produce ethereal sounds, while the wind players are asked to scrape various surfaces of their horns with bows. Sometimes these new requirements place unusual strains upon player's technical skills. In this latter composition of Kleinverstand, the trombone player must move his slide in and out with his right hand while he bows vigorously with his left. Resourceful use has also been made of the human voice by members of the avant guard. To perform one of his more famous compositions, *Das Schweinruf* (1974), Kleinverstand requires the singer to do research into certain arcane vocal practices native to rural Arkansas.

Not only do avant guard composers use conventional musical instruments in unconventional ways, they use unconventional sound sources for many of their compositions. As a good example of the lengths to which composers of our day go to achieve unique effects, we should describe a work by the eminent Italian composer, Giovanni Gabbia (1912-   ). His *Threnody for the Victims of Avant Guard Music* (1966) is a composition requiring outdoor performance in an arena the size

[21] It will also provide something of a shock for a person who has never heard any kind of a concert.

A 20th century composer about to perform his new concerto for bugle, beercans, and tape recorder.

of a football field. The work is scored for thirty-five jet engines lined up along one side of the field, sixty-eight diesel engines of two hundred horsepower each along the other side, three hundred sixty-two three-phase electric motors of ten horsepower each along one end, and three demolition teams each with two tons of TNT at the opposite end. The score is a complex interweaving of the four sound sources in such a fashion that at times they play alone, and at other times they play in complicated conjunction with one another. At the initial American performance of the work in the Houston Astrodome in August of 1978, failure to notify the civil authorities caused a panic among those outside the arena. The performance was interrupted by the arrival of a platoon of fire engines, twenty ambulances, and ten squadrons of riot police. All of this in no way violated the nature of the musical score. In fact, few members of the audience were even aware of the intrusions.

Avant guard composers have not been remiss in applying the science of electronics to the field of music. In fact some composers have limited their work solely to the field of electronic music. To become an electronic composer does not require flunking out from a major conservatory. All that is necessary is that one order a self-instructional course in radio and television repair from Popular Science Magazine and flunk that. As part of the instructional packages of such courses, one obtains a large amount of electronic equipment, which, if hooked up in strange and erratic ways, will produce strange and erratic sounds to suit the strange and erratic tastes of strange and erratic electronic composers. The electronic composer spends much of his time creating devices for producing particular classifications of sounds. Some of the more interesting devices, which by now have unfortunately become standardized are:

1) continuous static generator—a device providing the general background against which all electronic music is produced

2) white noise generator—a rarely employed device producing the only noise which is not injurious to the human ear

3) red noise generator—a device which produces such an excruciating sound that the hearer can see only the red portion of the visual spectrum

4) shriek amplifier—a device which transforms a modest human shriek into a grotesque, extraterrestrial horror

5) rumble filter—a device which filters out all but the lowest portion of the sound spectrum

Some 20th century compositional systems.

1. composer paints chicken's feet black and places chicken on manuscript paper. Voila!

2. facial tissues are preprinted with grand staff. As tissues are discarded, composer retrieves them and enters "collected data" in his notebooks.

3. composer, wearing rain-slicker, climbs upon a park statue and collects random bits of aleatoric material.

6) boom box—a device to amplify the signal from the rumble filter

7) sign wave generator—a device which produces a wavy, visual sign which notifies the audience of impending damage to the auditory nerves

8) variable howl synthesizer—a machine which can reproduce all manner of animal howling, at any frequency or with any frequency

9) tuneable lachrymotory signal amplifier—reproduces and amplifies the crying sounds of all creatures, great or small

10) solid-state grumble meter—a device which measures the audience reaction to electronic music.

Another application of technology to avant guard music has been in the use of the computer. Here the electronic composer connects his various sound producing devices to the computer, and then provides a program to set them into operation. There is a hope that second generation computers will be able to write their own programs, and hence the avant guard composer can be eliminated entirely from the process of making music.[22]

In most music employing the new electronic sounds and computer technology, an electronic tape replaces the conventional musical score. Performances of this music consist of sitting in front of tape recorders, amplifiers, and speakers and being bombarded by electronic noise. One will always find at these concerts stage hands who are willing to effect a total power blackout of the hall for a small fee. Look for them as you enter the hall; slip them a ten dollar bill; and you can escape the entire thing. Believe me, it will cost less than the physician's bill for repairing a punctured eardrum.

The French, who were responsible for much of avant guard music as well as some of World War II, have a vivid term for the various musical styles of these radical composers. By close analysis of the specific gravity of the brain cells of the avant guard, the French have determined that what is actually being produced is *musique concret.* The stubbornness with which these composers adhere to this silly nonsense is truly as concrete a phenomenon as one is likely to encounter in this ever-changing, contemporary world.

The twentieth century is not yet over, although there are certainly some of us who hope to

[22] Hope springs eternal in the human breast.

wake up in another age. In our century, as we have said, many have fled from modern music back to other eras which produced more compelling, emotional music. The audiences are not there, but the composers still are, flailing their arms[23] wildly and urging listeners to return. Is there hope for music in the future? In the final chapter of our study we must address this question.

[23] That is their machines, synthesizers, and tape recorders.

Chapter VIII

Hope for Music in the Future

Postface

In a work of this magnitude and depth, there are certainly many persons who contributed to its success, either willingly or unwillingly. To reduce the threat of lawsuit, it gives me pleasure to acknowledge my particular indebtedness to:

My students to whom the work is dedicated;

My colleagues, past and present, who passed on to me many of the textual tidbits contained herein, unaware that each was being programmed into the dark recesses of my mind to be used later for this arcane purpose;

My fellow musicologists, whose extensive studies of Mozarabic neumes have convinced me that entire lifetimes may be devoted to almost anything;

Peter Schickele, whose devoted musicological investigations, particularly into the life and works of P.D.Q. Bach, have proven for me an unattainable model;

My daughter, Cynthia, who read the manuscript, typed a large portion of it, suggested many additions, and counseled as many judicious deletions;

My wife, Sylvia, and my other daughter, Stephanie, who endured many hours at dinner listening to me laugh at myself;

Anita Hildebrandt, who, as she typed several chapters of the manuscript, was confused about the sanity of its author;

And finally to my publisher, who has risked economic disaster in undertaking such a project.

Frank J. Rocca

The illustrator of this book, Frank J. Rocca, has the dubious distinction of having been brought up in the same home town as Johnny Appleseed: Leominster, Massachusetts. This is probably just as well, since his education had to be completely discounted owing to the fact that he was well into his college years before it was discovered that he was holding his textbooks upside down. This left him with only one choice among the professions: he was forced to become an artist and a writer (specializing in unpublished fiction).

He also claims to be a musician, but this claim is as yet unsubstantiated by anyone, especially those who have heard him play the violin. A vast repository of thoroughly useless information, he was an ideal choice to work with the author on this book.

Mr. Rocca makes his home in two places, New York and Baltimore, fleeing from one to the other at opportune (necessary) strategic moments.

Photo Credit: Peter Sterns. Baltimore, Maryland